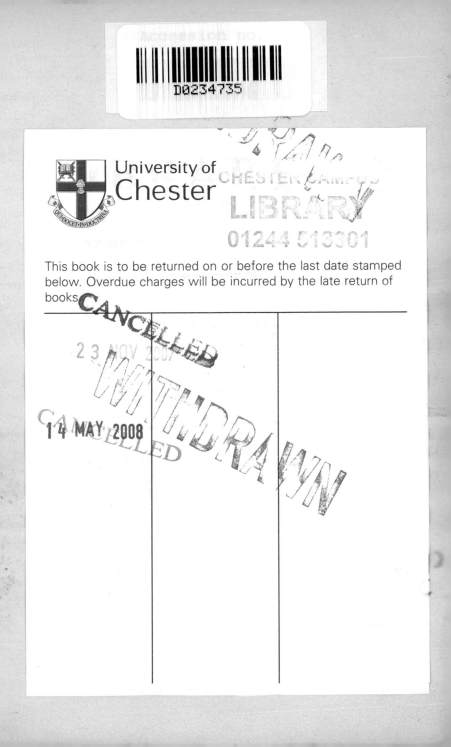

What is the New Age still saying to the Church?

John Drane

Marshall Pickering
An Imprint of HarperCollinsPublishers

Marshall Pickering is an imprint of
HarperCollins*Religious*
Part of HarperCollins*Publishers*
77-85 Fulham Palace Road, London W6 8JB

First published in Great Britain in 1991
by Marshall Pickering under the title
What is the New Age Saying to the Church?

This revised edition published in 1999

1 3 5 7 9 10 8 6 4 2

A catalogue record for this book is
available from the British Library.

ISBN 0 551 03194 8

Printed and bound in Great Britain by
Caledonian International Book Manufacturing Ltd, Glasgow

For Mark and Laura,
spiritual people for the new century

Contents

Preface

It is almost ten years since the first edition of this book appeared, under the title *What is the New Age Saying to the Church?* At the time, it took many Christians by surprise, for they had largely taken it for granted that, whatever the New Age might be, it was probably nothing that they needed to concern themselves with – and certainly not a movement from which they had anything to learn. Still, they bought it, and as my first readers pondered what I had to say, they began to find that it was resonating with their experience. Far from being an irrelevance to the apparently more important matters of evangelization and worship, it was actually raising key questions about how Christians might engage effectively with today's spiritual searchers in the New Age.

This was exactly what I had anticipated, for when I first encountered the New Age, it had challenged many of my own preconceptions not only about the nature of the church but also in relation to the ways that Christian theology has traditionally been articulated. In the intervening period, the New Age itself has changed, and in many respects has become almost coterminous with what we are now calling postmodernity. This revised edition of my book reflects that change of emphasis, and attempts to put the spirituality of our age within a slightly wider cultural context than was the case in the first edition. But while the details may have changed, the core concerns remain largely the same. One major change since the first edition is the way in which Western people have become less secretive about their spirituality, even in Britain which is sometimes thought of as a bastion of conservatism. Many church leaders were taken aback by the spontaneous public response to the death of Diana, Princess of Wales, in August 1997. But what happened then was absolutely consistent with the major trends of our culture. For some time there has been a growing movement towards a do-it-yourself spirituality which exhibits a robust disregard for religious establishments of all kinds, yet at the same time is rooted in traditions from the past, though expressed in ways that have immediate relevance to the felt needs of the day.

Have the churches heard what the New Age has been saying to them? Some have, but few seem to know how to do much about it. In Britain, at least, there is a kind of institutional paralysis in which 'the system' prevents even its own leading activists from pursuing the kind of innovations they believe in and know to be necessary. My analysis of what the church now needs to hear is naturally different from what I wrote a decade or so ago. In the intervening period, not only has the New Age changed in many respects, but so has the church. Throughout the Western world, but most especially in Europe (including Britain), it has declined quite significantly. People are voting with their feet and leaving the church, not because they are not interested in spiritual matters, but because – whether correctly or not – they perceive that the church is not interested in spirituality. Whereas ten years ago, young people were saying to me that the church was dull and boring, today they are more likely to dismiss the church as being unspiritual. For all these reasons, what I think the New Age is now saying is a good deal more radical than it was when I wrote the first edition of this book. As a result, though I have retained the same chapter structure as before, this has been a very considerable revision. No chapter remains the same as before, and four of them are so substantially rewritten that they are, in effect, completely new material.

One word that appears here with much greater frequency than before is 'spirituality'. Though this has become one of the buzz words of our culture, I find many Christians are confused by it, and some actively dislike it. This is partly due to the fact that it is a slippery word, capable of different meanings, which of course is also one of its attractions, because it can be infinitely expanded and redefined by those who use it. Still, it is here to stay, and even the British government's Department for Education and Employment has an official definition of 'spirituality': 'The valuing of the non-material aspects of life, and intimations of an enduring reality'. Another definition describes it as 'the inner experience of the individual when he [sic] senses a Beyond, especially as evidenced by the effect of this experience on his behavior when he actively attempts to harmonize his life with the Beyond'.[1] In this context, a majority of those who use this term tend to distinguish 'spirituality' from 'religion'. There is, obviously, a close connection between the two, which can perhaps be expressed by saying that, while all religion ought to be 'spiritual', not all 'spirituality' need be 'religious' in the sense of being a part of an identifiable faith tradition. One of the complaints of many New Agers, of course, is that many religions are not really 'spiritual'.

Though there is much that is new in this revised edition, all my observations here have been well rehearsed in seminars and workshops with churches of all traditions, and the warm response they have been given in those contexts encourages me to think they are still relevant to a wider readership. I meet many people who would desperately love to see the church reinvent itself in a form that will speak to the needs of today's people, but they frequently lack the courage to make the changes that will be necessary if that is to happen.

I am not naive enough to imagine that this book contains all the answers. It does not even contain all *my* answers, as readers will discover if they read it alongside my 1997 book *Faith in a Changing Culture.* Though the prognosis for the church's survival in Britain may look statistically bleak, I have every confidence that new ways of being church will emerge. Indeed, I know that this is already happening in scattered pockets around the world.

As before, my main source of information for this new edition has been New Agers themselves. I have been privileged to meet several of the world leaders of the movement, as well as attending many New Age exhibitions, and investigating at first hand the New Age psychological and medical therapies. All unattributed quotations are taken from conversations with such people. I have still not read many of the things that other Christians have written about the New Age, and that is reflected in my bibliographies and references. When I have occasionally read Christian expositions of the New Age, I have often found them tasteless, ill-informed and confrontational, which is another good reason for not referring to most of them, for in my view no useful purpose, either intellectual or spiritual, is served by quoting others merely to ridicule and dismiss them.

In recent years I have travelled extensively to observe and research the spiritual scene in the wider world. I have been particularly privileged to have visited California every year since 1992, for that is undoubtedly where the cutting edge of the New Age is to be found. But it is now a global phenomenon, and its popularity can as readily be seen in Australia, New Zealand, and South-East Asia, as well as closer to home on the streets of Britain and Europe. Travelling to the non-Western world has only served to strengthen my conviction, expressed in the preface to the first edition, that much within the New Age – and more widely within postmodern culture – is a form of Western intellectual imperialism, which is just as much a challenge to some contemporary Christian practices as it is to our inherited culture patterns generally.

Many people helped in the writing of the first edition of this book, and in sharpening my thinking and challenging my personal spirituality in the intervening years. They include groups in universities, colleges, seminaries and churches across the world, members of various New Age organizations, owners of New Age resource centres, and therapists of all kinds. As always, my wife and partner, Olive, has made a particular contribution to my thinking, not least as we have worked together in teaching courses related to contemporary spirituality, and working out for ourselves how best to model the values of the Gospel in an ever-changing cultural context. In the process, we have travelled the world together, but more importantly we have journeyed alongside one another in seeking to follow Jesus – and that, for me, will always be at the heart of any relevant spirituality for this generation.

John Drane

Chapter One

Mapping out the Territory

Ten years ago, hardly anyone in Britain had heard of it. Today, most people are at least familiar with the term 'New Age', even if they have little idea what it means. Most high street bookstores have substantial New Age (or Body, Mind and Soul) sections, while specialist shops abound, offering goods whose purpose could loosely be described as 'spiritual'. The 'New Age' label is used to advertise consumer products ranging from beauty care and fashions to music and 'alternative' health care. New Age thinking and terminology have permeated into every significant area of life. Its concepts are taken for granted as the raw materials from which the plots for Hollywood blockbusters are crafted, and right across the world it has become one of the most frequently discussed subjects on TV chat shows. It has generated a whole new style of 'New Age music', and it can scarcely be denied that the New Age has taken the entertainment scene and the media by storm.

Nor is the influence of New Age thinking restricted to the popular culture of marketing and television, for there is no shortage of evidence of New Age influence and insights being brought to bear on many academic disciplines. The ranks of New Age writers include scientists,[1] as well as social scientists and business professors – while the emergence of transpersonal psychology as a major 'fourth force' in that discipline is, according to many of its practitioners, an integral part of the New Age movement.[2] New Age devotees include lawyers and sober-suited business people doing self-improvement courses and using overtly spiritual techniques for handling corporate stress management, wealth creation and relationship and communication training. Even major UK public institutions have on occasion been known to promote the New Age quite overtly,[3] while some educational institutions take New Age concepts as the underlying philosophy for their courses. In England, the old Lancashire mill town of Skelmersdale is the unlikely home for the Maharishi School of the Age of Enlightenment. Here children aged from 3 to 16 study using the Unified Field Education System, based on a theoretical concept called The Science of Creative Intelligence. Spiritual therapies and techniques form part of the everyday curriculum and help create an atmosphere which, it is claimed, makes the children more relaxed in relating to staff, and more willing to learn. If they go on to higher education, children from schools like this may find the California Institute of Integral Studies in San Francisco a good place to be. Its catalogue of degree programmes lists courses on all kinds of esoteric religious topics, including Shamanic Art and Ritual Healing; Nutrition and Spiritual Growth; The Re-Emergence of the Goddess; Voice, Psyche and Spirit; Learning to Heal. Even ostensibly mainstream, 'secular' educators can be found experimenting with claims that the performance of school children can be improved by techniques that range from breathing and relaxation exercises through to fantasy games, yoga, transcendental meditation and making contact with 'spirit guides'. Alongside all this, fitness freaks have developed a bewildering array of unconventional health cures and psychological therapies.

Searching for Definitions

It is easy enough to use the term 'New Age' as a convenient label for all these things, and more like them. But what exactly is it? And why does it matter? These may seem the most obvious questions to ask – and in that order. Finding satisfactory answers is, however, not so easy. Indeed, there is no one simple answer that will explain everything that seems to be encompassed by the New Age phenomenon. Some have argued that there is no such thing as the New Age, and regard it as an artificial construct of paranoid Christian fundamentalists, who with the collapse of Communism no longer had anything to hate, and therefore needed to create a mythical enemy for themselves.[4] Even those who happily bear the 'New Age' label sometimes seem unable to define it. Social psychologist John L. Simmons admits that 'I knew something was stirring in the world but I didn't know what', and then proceeds to make grandiose claims that

> the signs of the new movement are everywhere ... millions of people are, in one way or another, becoming unofficially involved in it ... [its findings] may currently be the most vital information in the world, with incredible implications for every man, woman, and child alive today.[5]

At the same time, however, others who once thought they knew what it was, and who happily wore the New Age label, now wish to discard it. Kenny Kaufman, producer of San Francisco's annual *Whole Life Expo*, is one of them. 'It was OK in the '70s to say "New Age",' he explains, 'but now people think "rip-off" when they see New Age. So we're now calling it the new era of awareness.'[6] Hemitra Crecraft and Sue King, who caused a stir among the conservative inhabitants of Pennsylvania when they first opened their Chester County New Age emporium, also admit

'We don't even call ourselves New Age,' adding: 'it has the conno-
tation of the occult.'[7] Hollywood superstar and leading New Age
activist Shirley Maclaine expresses a similar sentiment.

> *Millions of people all over the world are so interested in this*
> *stuff that they support an entire industry of books, teachings,*
> *schools, individuals, and literature of all kinds devoted to the*
> *metaphysical dimensions of life. I wouldn't call it the occult …*
> *I would call it an interest in the spiritual dimension of life.*[8]

On the other side of the Atlantic, Carol Riddell of Scotland's Findhorn Community agrees:

> *We are now a little wary of this description, which was once*
> *eagerly embraced by the Findhorn Community, because in pop-*
> *ular thought it has become connected with the sensation seekers*
> *… whose interest lies less in seeking spiritual transformation*
> *than in dabbling in the occult, or in practising classical capi-*
> *talist entrepreneurship on the naive.*[9]

One obvious way to try and identify the New Age is to look for
empirical signs of its presence in our culture, but this too can be a
misleading approach, for it embraces an extraordinary diversity of
artefacts, beliefs, techniques and methods of devotion whose purpose can all be described as vaguely 'spiritual'. In the *Blue Pages* –
a New Age equivalent of the *Yellow Pages*, published by Prasada
Hamilton in Western Australia – colour analysts rub shoulders
with transpersonal psychologists and New Age musicians, while
university courses in consciousness studies compete for clients
alongside Eastern gurus and Gnostic priests, all of them offering
personal transformation and self-discovery through therapies that
range from traditional homeopathic medicine through to healing
with crystals, past-life recall and advice from entities channelled in

from outer space or some other spirit world. Alongside such concerns for personal development is a deep-seated anxiety for the future of our polluted planet – a commitment that may be expressed through actions ranging from regular membership of an environmental pressure group to life-changing pilgrimages to remote deserts and mountainsides, spiritual communication with dolphins and whales, or involvement with any one of a multitude of rituals designed to enhance attunement to Gaia, the earth goddess. Then there are the electronic gadgets that are reputed to have the power to make anyone who uses them into a new person by reorienting their brainwaves, not to mention the infinite number of ever-changing combinations of therapy and massage that will allegedly do the same thing for their bodies. One therapist I came across was even offering to channel messages from Barbie dolls, which she described as 'the polyethylene essence who is 700 million teaching entities'.[10] On a recent visit to Venice Beach in southern California, I encountered a New Age teacher claiming that 'Surgical abortions are now unnecessary: women no longer need to be the victim of physical pain', and advising them 'Don't allow the ignorance of the patriarchy to make unchangeable choices for you.' The alternative he offered was 'pregnancy dissolvement' which, it was claimed, is a natural 'spiritual' therapeutic for terminating unplanned pregnancies.[11]

It is a major challenge even to describe something so multifaceted, let alone to analyse it in any systematic way. This is not a problem for New Agers, who for other reasons are generally contemptuous of analytical knowledge. For those who still need some rational way to understand things, one philosophical option would be to invoke Wittgenstein's notion of 'family resemblances' as a way of understanding how such apparently disparate elements can all belong on the same spectrum of belief and lifestyle.[12] A social science perspective might suggest it could variously be described as a 'metanetwork', or network of networks,[13] or a SPIN (segmented polycentric integrated network).[14]

Put in a different way, anyone trying to define the New Age is faced with the same problem as the blind beggars who tried to describe an elephant. One, starting from the animal's legs, described it as a tree; another, grasping its trunk, assumed it must be a hose; while the third, taking hold of its tail, insisted that an elephant was like a rope. They were all correct, of course, but none of them had the complete picture. The New Age is the same. A New Age music catalogue, for instance, might contain recordings channelled in from some spiritual world, which will allegedly put listeners into altered states of consciousness as they are played. But it might just as easily contain Gregorian chant and the music of contemporary Christian songwriter Graham Kendrick. What is true of the parts is not necessarily going to be true of the whole (and vice versa). In reality, the only thing these particular examples have in common is that someone put them in the same catalogue and labelled them all 'New Age'! But the self-understanding either of monks singing medieval chants or of Christians playing Kendrick worship songs would generally be totally unrelated to any so-called New Age philosophy.

I remember struggling with this kind of evident confusion when I first became interested in trying to understand the New Age. Sitting with an African-American basketball coach over breakfast one day at a homely coffee shop in Piedmont, California, I asked him for his opinion of what is going on here. After a long period of reflection, my companion put it like this: 'Think of the New Age movement as a vacuum cleaner,' he said. 'It picks up whatever is there, and messes it all up. So when you open the bag, you recognize all the bits and pieces that are in there – but the mixture is completely different from anything you've ever seen before, or anything you could even imagine. You probably wonder how it can all possibly belong together. The fact is, it doesn't.

Those things are in there just because the vacuum cleaner happened to pick them up. If it had moved in a different direction, it would have sucked all kinds of other things in. They would look quite unlike the first collection – but they would be "New Age" as well.'

Whatever image we use to describe it, the New Age is at heart an essentially eclectic phenomenon. In her history of the Findhorn Foundation, Carol Riddell describes life there as 'a spiritual supermarket, with all kinds of different "products" on the shelves to sample'.[15] She provides a bewildering list of what these products might include: Buddhism, hatha yoga, ta'i chi, Sufism, transcendental meditation, organic food, past-life therapy, *A Course in Miracles*, as well as various elements from the Christian mystical tradition – all of which, she comments, 'makes up what has been described as the "New Age" movement'.[16] In this supermarket of spiritual and emotional goodies, customers may choose whatever they think will meet their needs. Since personal needs will vary from one stage of life to another, even in some cases from one day to the next, the exact range of goods is constantly changing. Much – if not all – of them, far from being new, are actually recycled from the past, and represent the recovery of a lot of very old spiritual nostrums that have been either lost or marginalized over the years. This has been partly the result of the influence of the great religions, especially the Judeo-Christian tradition in the West, but it is also due to the unthinking acceptance of a secular or unspiritual worldview within Western culture more generally. For decades, if not centuries, people have been told that the world is not a sacred or mystical place, but can be explained quite simply by the discoveries of modern science and the understanding of laws of nature. Nowadays, people are not so sure, and increasing numbers are searching for spiritual explanations of what is going on. After two centuries or more of radical scepticism about anything religious, it has suddenly become trendy to be spiritual again. It should not have surprised anyone when, following the tragic and unexpected death of Diana, Princess of Wales, in August 1997, a significant proportion of British people – not to mention huge numbers in other places around the world – expressed their response through practices that, on any definition, can only be described as religious. Not only in London, but throughout even the smallest villages in Britain, people prayed openly in the streets. They built shrines, which became sites of pilgrimage and at which they burned candles as they invoked the memory and name of Diana, while seeking to explore the meaning of their own lives in the context of the loss of hers. Others held what was effectively a vigil by their TV sets for a full week, as the story unfolded in all its grim details.[17] In the months following the tragedy, it was only a matter of time before 'The Church of Diana' would emerge, with its own 'Bible' supposedly based on revelations channelled in from Diana's spirit in another world by Chairman Yao.[18]

Though it has religious manifestations, the New Age is definitely not a religion. It is not even a belief system in the traditional sense, and certainly not a cult. There is nothing to join. It is sometimes referred to as a 'movement', but that too is a misnomer, for the New Age is not even a recognizable pressure group. There is no headquarters, and New Age devotees can be found engaging in a wide variety of practices, many of them incompatible with things that other New Agers might be doing. The only sense in which it is a 'movement' is that it is, quite literally, moving and changing its shape all the time. As the preface to every issue of *Common Ground* puts it:

> *there are undoubtedly as many paths to personal transformation as there are people … Whether a resource is useful to your personal transformation is a matter of attunement: it's a matter of resonance between what the resource is and who you are at this moment in time.*

This inherent instability within the New Age itself makes it all the more essential that we establish a clear frame of reference within which to understand it all. Without this, the most we can hope for would be to produce a comprehensive listing of the many ideas, teachings and groups which tend to identify with this label, despite their obvious lack of real connection with one another. This is one of the reasons why some commentators question whether there really is such a thing as the New Age at all, and argue that what we now call by this name is just, as one person put it to me, 'the sweepings of the ages'. Certainly, one of the major weaknesses of many books on the subject is the tendency to present phenom- enological descriptions of belief systems and therapies as if their meaning is self-evident, rather than trying to identify the underly- ing cultural concerns which have led to the emergence of this spirituality at this point in Western history. The phenomena are important, and appropriate analysis of them can illuminate significant aspects of the New Age spiritual search. Indeed, in later chapters of this book we will consider some specific examples of such things. However, if the focus is exclusively on that, the most we can hope for is to catalogue and list many of the things that are going on in today's spiritualities, but without any clear perception of what it might all mean, particularly for the traditional source of Western spirituality, in the Christian churches.[19] At the outset, therefore, I want first to ask why all this is happening now, and to suggest that when, in the light of our answer to that, we then return to examine some of the empirical evidence of the New Age we will be better equipped both to understand what is going on, and also to appreciate the full force of just what this might all be saying to the churches.

Putting the New Age in Context

In study of the New Age, there have been three dominant explanations of its rise to prominence. These may be described as religious, sociological and cultural. The religious explanation begins from the obvious fact that some significant strands in the New Age seem closely related to, if not identical with, major world religions, especially those connected with India, such as Hinduism and Buddhism, but also including aspects of other Asian faith systems like Taoism. An attractive, though ultimately unsatisfactory, explanation of the New Age is that it is the product of what happens when Eastern traditions travel west. It is certainly true that there is today a much greater awareness of and appreciation for non-Western faiths than would have been the case a century ago, when most Western people were in total ignorance of how the rest of the world lived and believed. But this interest has largely been engendered by Western people themselves, and in spite of claims to the contrary there really is no evidence at all to suggest that the leaders of non-Christian faiths are engaging in the kind of proselytizing that Christians have historically pursued. If there is more interest in religions such as Hinduism and Buddhism today, that is not because Hindus and Buddhists are trying to promote themselves, but because Western people are discovering gaps in their own spirituality which, many believe, non-Western worldviews are better equipped to address. One can, of course, also identify certain strands in Western thinking that have surfaced from time to time through the ages, and that can more easily be integrated with Eastern traditions than with traditional Christianity. Aldous Huxley highlighted the persistence of what he called 'the perennial philosophy', manifested in, for example, Western mystical traditions such as Gnosticism, Freemasonry, Rosicrucianism, Theosophy, Romanticism, Transcendentalism, and so on, and more recently Robert Ellwood has proposed that 'the New Age is a contemporary manifestation of a western alternative spirituality tradition going back at least to the Greco-Roman world [which] ... flows like an underground river through the Christian centuries, breaking into high visibility in the Renaissance'.[20] There is no doubt that the naturalistic worldview represented by such groups has always had many similar emphases to those found in Eastern religions, but these have historically been minority interests mostly confined to the intellectual and social elite. They never had any chance of coming to the fore in Western culture for as long as the traditional ideology, mediated through the Christian story, remained dominant. Insofar as the New Age is a rediscovery of these things, as well as a new interest in non-Western religious traditions, this has been brought about not by some natural development in the history of religions, but by the collapse of the underlying ideological foundation which for centuries has given coherence to the Western world. To see the New Age as only, or even predominantly, an aspect of the history of religions is to miss the point of what is happening.

Another way of interpreting the emergence of the New Age is to see it as an essentially sociological phenomenon, related specifically and directly to the growing instability of life in today's world, as the old ways of doing things change and the new seem less certain and secure than what they are replacing. There is no doubt that the rate of change in the lives of us all has accelerated in recent decades, and things that once seemed set to last for ever are now seen as transient influences in an ever-revolving scene. Even the world map has been redrawn in the light of the collapse of the Soviet empire, as new countries have come into existence and long-buried tribal loyalties have surfaced again. Economic stability seems as elusive as it ever was, while increasing numbers of people have little time even for the politicians whom they elect into office, and there is a growing sense that the establishment cannot be trusted any more. In its extreme form, this has led to the emergence of militia groups all across the USA. Their membership is tiny, though many more people are convinced that there is a major international cover-up relating to the sighting of UFOs and alleged extra-terrestrial visitations to the earth. At a more mundane level, job security is no longer what it once was, while home and family life are increasingly fragile for most people. All that, coupled with the fact that we are at the beginning of the new millennium, combines to make this an uncertain and threatening time to be alive, as we all seem to have less and less power even over our own lives.

In this context, what more natural thing to do than seek new ways of regaining such lost power, especially when that can be tailor-made for the individual, through esoteric spiritual experiences that by definition cannot be accessible to all and sundry? This is undoubtedly one of the major motivations behind the rapid growth of management courses based on 'spiritual' principles, as we shall see in a later chapter. But the New Age also claims to offer to ordinary people the key to a better, more fulfilled life, empowering them to be the best they can at a time when the rest of the system can seem to be undermining their prospects for a happy life. Viewed in this way, the New Age can be understood as the religious and personal equivalent of the resurgent nationalism that is making such an impact in the political sphere, though the New Age is a response not only to over-centralized governments but also – and more especially – to paternalistic and inflexible religious systems, that can often seem (particularly to those outside them) to be more interested in their own power than in the personal spiritual development even of their own adherents. This is certainly a widely held opinion of the church, and in this setting the New Age offers a do-it-yourself spirituality in the midst of a do-it-yourself world, as people take responsibility for their own lives, often because they have been exploited and oppressed by the people they thought they should have been able to trust. Many of those attracted to the New Age are people who have been damaged by their involvement with the church, particularly (though not exclusively) women who find themselves excluded by patriarchal structures.

These are all serious issues, and we shall return to them later. But they are not sufficient by themselves to explain the rise of the New Age at this time, which is why I want to propose that both the religious and the sociological evidences are actually part of a much larger cultural change, and it is this which lies at the root of the New Age's popularity. In many ways, it is a pity that the term 'New Age' has persisted as a way of describing what is going on, for the use of such an expression can give the impression that it is nothing more than the concern of a few minority groups. The reality, however, is quite different. Not surprisingly, those who are still firmly committed to the inherited rationalist-materialist worldview of Western culture tend to regard the New Age with both amazement and disbelief. A return to superstition, mythology and spirituality on this scale is the very last thing that should be taking place at the beginning of the twenty-first century in a culture supposedly dominated by the mindset of scientific technology. In reality, though, 'New Age ideas and activities are now virtually co-extensive with western culture'.[21]

So what is going on? The simple answer is that we are witnessing the end of a civilization. Or, to use a different term much favoured in the New Age, our culture is undergoing a paradigm shift. We are at a *kairos* moment in history, and what is happening today will in due course prove to be as significant as the discovery by Copernicus that the solar system was not geocentric but heliocentric, or Newton's articulation of laws of nature, or Einstein's promulgation of the theory of relativity. A growing consensus of opinion believes that the culture and worldview that had its origins in the European Enlightenment – and beyond that, of course, in the Reformation and classical Greece and Rome – is now in a state of terminal collapse. While the new paradigm is still in the process of formation, its exact form will remain indistinct, which is why it looks incoherent and chaotic at present. New Agers are not the only ones to believe that the prevailing culture is changing, and a comprehensive account of the shift from modernity to what is now being called postmodernity would take us well beyond the narrow concerns of religious and theological enquiry, to embrace science as well as politics and financial disciplines. But it is becoming evident that what we have hitherto called the New Age is, in effect, the religious manifestation of postmodernity, and as such it is part of the questioning and redefining of the values and methods inherited from the European Enlightenment that has swept through all areas of intellectual reflection in the last twenty years or so.[22]

As such, the various threads that go to make up the New Age tapestry are held together not by a common ideology, but by a shared perception of the nature of contemporary cultural change. The New Age's answer to the dislocation and collapse now facing Western culture is that the only way forward will be through a transformational shift in consciousness, of cosmic proportions. As with many critiques of modernity (including Christian ones), the New Age is itself a product of this same worldview with which it expresses dissatisfaction, though unlike other critiques it also unashamedly searches for solutions in what can only be described as a 'pre-modern' worldview, based on a prescientific, essentially mythological epistemology.[23] This close connection of the New Age to postmodernity should be sufficient to alert us to the difficulty of finding easy answers to many of the questions we may have about it. Ernest Gellner's perceptive study of postmodernism sums up the feelings of many who are struggling to interpret the present intellectual climate: 'Postmodernism is a contemporary movement. It is strong and fashionable. Over and above this, it is not altogether clear what the devil it is. In fact, clarity is not conspicuous amongst its marked attributes.'[24]

Nevertheless, some things are clear enough, among them the kind of understanding of Western cultural history that is likely to be held by a majority of today's spiritual searchers, who would typically put forward an argument along the following lines:

Our present predicament can be traced mostly to mistakes made by Western thinkers in the course of the last 500 years, which in turn was rooted in the West's love affair with the rationality of the Greeks. This philosophy has led to the marginalization of human and spiritual values, and an unhealthy preoccupation with a mechanistic, rationalist, reductionist worldview. There has been a profound loss of spiritual perception, and to resolve the present crisis that trend needs to be reversed. The recovery of spirituality must be a top priority. Traditional Western sources of spiritual guidance will, however, be of little help in this process: the Christian church is inextricably bound up with the old cultural establishment, so much so that the defective Enlightenment worldview was, in effect, little more than the logical outcome of classical Christian beliefs and values.

Inevitably, this analysis is not applied in practice with a great deal of rigour or intellectual consistency, for in reality virtually no one would wish to turn the clock back to a pre-scientific age. Like many others, New Agers have a love–hate relationship with modern culture. On the one hand, it has led to enormous advances in, for example, transportation systems and medical science. But the prevailing opinion is that, in spite of its very tangible benefits, the disadvantages ultimately tip the scales in the other direction. The golden coin of modern progress has a heavily tarnished reverse side. The old mechanistic models of understanding human life frequently seem to have created more problems than they have solved. In conjunction with a reductionist approach to knowledge, a rationalist-materialist outlook has created discontinuities in every area of life, from the depersonalization experienced by patients within modern scientific medicine to the pollution of the environment. Things are getting worse, not better. The great promise of Enlightenment philosophy and science was that it would enable people to control the environment, rather than the environment controlling them. But today's environmental crisis has unleashed forces that no amount of human reason will be able to control, and for the first time since the Middle Ages people's ultimate future destiny seems to be in the control of unknown, and probably unknowable, natural forces. Within this frame of reference, there is an inevitability to the conclusion reached by physicist Fritjof Capra, who links these matters to new insights within his own discipline:

> *The new concepts in physics have brought about a profound change in our world view; from the mechanistic conception of Descartes and Newton to a holistic or ecological view, a view which I have found to be similar to the views of mystics of all ages and traditions.*[25]

What this means for the Western Christian tradition is all too obvious. The ills of the present are blamed on a loss of direction by previous generations. Inspired by a rationalist-materialist-reductionist worldview, our forebears lost sight of some important dimensions of the human situation. Spiritual and personal values were ignored, and even denied, in favour of a mechanistic viewpoint. If, then, a loss of spiritual perception was a key cause of the problem, the recovery of spirituality will be crucial for any effective resolution of our present plight. On the face of it, this might sound like good news for the church, and from one angle indeed it is, for at least it puts spirituality firmly on the public agenda. But it has a powerful sting in the tail, and Christians who wish to engage in serious dialogue with the New Age will first have to face some potentially unpalatable facts about themselves. For a widely held assumption is that, if there is a way out of the mess, then traditional Western sources of spiritual guidance will be of no help in finding it. Put simply, the Christian church is a part of the old cultural establishment that actually created the present predicament. Consequently, it is so tainted by inadequate and unsatisfactory metaphysical understandings that it is incapable of exercising any constructive role in charting a new course for the future. Most New Agers have no difficulty in drawing a straight line from the Enlightenment to the church, and when one part of the philosophical edifice begins to crumble, that inevitably places major question-marks against all its other central components. Either way, the practical outcome is the same: if Christianity is part of the problem it cannot also be part of the solution. Consequently, the only place to find useful spiritual guidance will be in other cultures and worldviews, or within ourselves – and both of these play a significant part in New Age spirituality.

The relationship between Christianity, the Enlightenment and Western culture is not quite that simple, of course. It can be debated whether Christian values shaped the Enlightenment, or whether it was the other way round and the church allowed itself to be taken over by essentially secular values.[26] But in the New Age, as in postmodernity more generally, image and perception is everything, and once something is believed by a sufficient number of people, it becomes irrelevant whether or not it is historically accurate or literally true. For better or worse, therefore, Christianity is increasingly perceived as part of the problem, and for that reason it cannot also be part of the solution: if spirituality is to be restored to today's world, it will have to come from somewhere else.

Mapping the New Age Landscape

We have already seen that the New Age can hold together beliefs
and practices that, on conventional definitions of rationality,
would be regarded as incompatible, logically contradictory and
mutually self-exclusive. For that reason alone, it is pointless to try
and construct a detailed route map through all the intricacies of
New Age spirituality. Nevertheless, it is perfectly feasible to identify some fundamental compass points that can provide a general
sense of direction through the New Age maze, without being pre-
scriptive about the actual path that any given New Ager might
actually follow. I want to propose that there are four dominant
polarities through which transformational philosophies and experiences are presently being pursued within the New Age, and that
virtually every current belief and practice belongs to one or more
of these categories.

Moving East: Non-Western Worldviews

That is, the traditional worldviews of Eastern religions. An attractive, if superficial, view states that, if the cause of our present
predicament rests in things that are modern and Western, then the
way to resolve it will be to seek solutions in things that are ancient
and Eastern (or at least, not Western in the traditional sense). As
has already been pointed out, many Western people are committing themselves to Eastern spiritual paths for this reason, particularly – but not exclusively – Buddhism, albeit in a Westernized
form. We will explore the way in which Eastern spirituality is being
Westernized in a later chapter, but Shirley Maclaine expresses a
popular opinion when she comments that 'this New Age is the
time when the intuitive beliefs of the East and the scientific thinking of the West could meet and join – the twain wed at last'.[27]

Moving Sideways: First-nation Beliefs

Long before white Westerners settled in the Americas or Australasia, these lands – and others like them – were home to ancient nations. The environmentally friendly lifestyles of these people were brutally suppressed, and their spirituality was devalued by Western colonists who labelled it 'primitive' and 'unscientific'. With the benefit of hindsight, it now seems that Western people could have learned much from the traditional lifestyles of aboriginal peoples. Could it therefore be that by reaffirming these values that were previously discarded, the world's peoples together might find new ways to take us forward into the future? In the process, white Westerners might also expiate some of the guilt they now feel for the behaviour of their forebears. This has become a major concern within the New Age, and bookstores are bulging with books on topics like native American spirituality, while today's New Agers can often be found reconstructing the medicine wheels and other spiritual artefacts which their forebears took such delight in destroying only a century ago.

Moving Back: Nature-focused Spirituality

Long before the spread of classical 'Western' values, articulated through the categories of Greek philosophy and spread by the power of Christendom, Europe itself was home to a different, arguably more spiritual worldview. Should Western people not therefore be looking for answers within their own heritage, by the rediscovery and appropriation of the kind of worldview that inspired and motivated their own distant ancestors? This concern accounts for the burgeoning interest in neo-paganism in its many forms, which is one of the fastest-growing aspects of New Age spirituality in northern Europe today.[28]

Going Within: Person-centred Spirituality

Many of those who today are searching for new ways of being have no interest at all in anything that could be called 'religion'. The development of psychotherapies of various kinds – not least the rise of transpersonal psychology – is providing this kind of 'secular' person with access to the same kind of transformational experiences as mystical religious traditions offer, without the initially unwelcome baggage of religious dogma. Hence the popularity of transformational video- and audio-tapes, bodywork and other therapies – often supported by claims that modern physics and mathematics are now 'proving' the value of all this in some kind of scientific sense.

Unity and Diversity

The unique forms of New Age spirituality emerge from the interweaving of these different and ostensibly unrelated threads. But while diversity is a key empirical hallmark of the New Age, not all New Agers are equally supportive of the attempt to construct an eclectic worldview from such widely assorted materials. David Spangler and William Irwin Thomson are typical of those who welcome the self-conscious merging of different traditions:

> *This new planetary sensibility or culture will be less a thing and more a process that nourishes our creativity and wholeness and provides sustenance for building the bodies of tomorrow ... we are reimagining our world. We are taking hunks of ecology and slices of science, pieces of politics and a sprinkle of economics, a pinch of religion and a dash of philosophy, and we are reimagining these and a host of other ingredients into something new: a New Age, a reimagination of the world.*[29]

Others are less convinced by this approach. Starhawk, for example, writes disdainfully of people who are spiritually starved in their own culture and 'unwittingly become spiritual strip miners damaging other cultures in superficial attempts to uncover their mystical treasures'.[30] Carol Riddell sounds a similar warning:

> *It is as if we were in a market place with many stalls offering goods. Some people go to one stall to buy, others go to another. We support each other constantly,* but the path of inner transformation is ultimately a personal one. However much we may share with others, each of us has a unique path to the Self.[31]

One of the mistakes frequently made by Christians is to ignore or downplay the extent to which there is theological and ideological diversity within the whole New Age spectrum. For example, in the first edition of this book, in my enthusiasm to identify hard-and-fast categories with which to understand the New Age, I myself mistakenly supposed that one of its universal characteristics is an essentially monistic worldview, in which 'all is one'. That understanding frequently leads to a form of pantheism, in which all things also become 'God', imbued with the same energy or life force. It is now clear, however, that at least two quite different worldviews can be identified within the New Age, one of which certainly is monistic, while the other is strongly dualistic, though set within a framework that has some connections with a sort of monism.[32] The first has strong historical connections to the kind of creation-centred pantheism of the English Romantic poets such as Wordsworth, Shelley and Blake, and to the similar Transcendentalist movement in North America, typified by Muir, Thoreau and Emerson. The second has been strongly represented in Britain by Sir George Trevelyan, with his neo-Gnostic insistence that, far from salvation being found in this world, it can only come through some decisive intervention from beyond.[33] This view would be shared by others who claim to be in communication with beings from other worlds, and who channel messages from spirit guides and extra-terrestrials, or speculate about the lost continents of Lemuria and Atlantis, or legends of Arthurian Britain.

As we now focus on different aspects of the New Age, it is important to bear in mind that what unites these diverse beliefs and therapies is not some clearly articulated worldview or ideology that is common to them all, but the simple conviction that the culture of modernity has got it wrong, and we now need to search wherever we will in order to discover new ways of putting things right. The key test of that is practical effectiveness, not ideological consistency. It is understandable that we will want to come up with some all-embracing definition of what constitutes the New Age, but the amazing diversity of the ingredients that go into its eclectic spiritual mixture will always ensure that any definition we produce can, with perfectly good reason, be challenged by someone else, whose experience of the phenomenon has been quite different. The New Age is like a movie with a constantly changing plot, being produced by a director who writes the script only after the filming is completed. What is presented in the following chapters is a series of stills from the larger movie – or, if you prefer the image I used earlier, of different bits gathered up in the cultural vacuum cleaner. They do not tell the whole story, but they will highlight some of the significant ingredients.

Chapter Two

What is the New Age?

It is not difficult to get lost in exploring this subject, and with such a diverse assortment of spiritual goodies on sale at the New Age store, most customers visiting for the first time find themselves totally mesmerized by it all. Even those who call in regularly find the dazzling display very difficult to describe to others. Understanding the New Age can feel like trying to wrestle with a jelly. No sooner does it seem to be in control than the shape of the whole thing changes and it becomes necessary to start again. For many people, that is precisely its attraction. There is so much to explore that it is almost impossible to get bored. New Agers would certainly have no trouble agreeing with the eighteenth-century British poet William Cowper, who once wrote

> *Variety's the very spice of life*
> *That gives it all its flavour*

The New Age gives the spiritual searcher freedom to choose from a whole range of possibilities, without necessarily making a specific commitment to any of them. Here, as elsewhere, fashions and fads come and go. A typical New Ager will maybe become fascinated by the mysticism of the Sufis, and that will last for a while. Then he or she may move on to certain forms of healing therapy or physical bodywork – something like Reiki, aromatherapy, acupuncture or Rolfing, perhaps. Reincarnation could then suddenly become flavour of the month, until past-life recall therapies are discovered, or messages allegedly 'channelled' from entities in some other world begin to look attractive. Various aspects of Christian belief may also be sucked in and added to this heady mixture of pop spirituality.

No matter what a person's needs may be, they can almost certainly find somebody somewhere who will have the answer to them. A 1998 ad for *The Cosmic Shaman* offers clients

> *a unique combination of inner child work, Shamanic ritual, visualizations, spiritual healing and energy releasing ... Shamanic soul retrieval, ear coning, alien abduction, implant clearing, apprenticeship training, goddess rituals, entity removal, aromatherapy, earth tribe essential oils ... [which will result in] you being cleared (mentally, physically, emotionally, spiritually – from this lifetime and past lives) from whatever is blocking you from having the life you so richly deserve.*

Another advert in the same journal offers a similar service for pets:

> *teaching animals to make the most appropriate choices possible, to live in harmony and wholeness within themselves and their human counterparts ... personal growth for you and your animal companion ... creating a relationship and a way of being together that encompasses mutual love, compassion, understanding, respect, and listening as a way of life.*[1]

With all this – and more – on offer, the possibilities are obviously both fascinating and endless. Some of the problems involved in pinning down the New Age movement have already been outlined, and adverts like this provide good illustrations of the difficulties we are likely to face. Nevertheless, some key elements do keep recurring, and it is possible to use them to sketch out some of the New Age's main characteristics.

The Age of Aquarius

The New Age is often referred to as the Age of Aquarius. This terminology is taken from an ancient astrological timetable related to the signs of the Zodiac, according to which the Age of Aries (the bull) would be followed by the Age of Pisces (the fish), which in turn will be superseded by the arrival of a new age, the Age of Aquarius (the water bearer). The present Age of Pisces roughly corresponds with the Christian era, and its characteristics have mostly been things which would be better forgotten – division, war, injustice, hatred, mistrust and bigotry. It is often claimed that these have been produced by the dualistic separation between God and humanity that is at the heart of Judeo-Christian belief. Indeed, some correlate these astrological ages with the dispensations of law, grace and freedom into which the medieval theologian Joachim of Fiore (1135–1202) divided world history, and then go on to identify Aries with the Father (Judaism), Pisces with the Son (Christianity) and Aquarius with the Spirit (New Age). By contrast with all that has preceded it, the Age of Aquarius will usher in a time of peace, harmony, wholeness and restoration – for people, and ultimately for the whole universe. At this time, people and God will be reunified, there will be a healing of all the separation and a rediscovery of the oneness of all things. As a result, the New Age is not about domination or competition, but about co-operation. People are looking to see where they belong, and where they might connect with other aspects of the cosmos. In the process they are discovering that humankind is not actually at the mercy of some objective forces arraigned against them out there, but that the only real energy is within ourselves. The only reality we experience is what we create ourselves. If we all create our own reality, then by focusing on wholeness and health instead of worrying about disasters and failures, we can together create something entirely new, that will be better than what has gone before. As Marilyn Ferguson puts it:

> *The paradigm of the Aquarian conspiracy sees humankind embedded in nature. It promotes the autonomous individual in a decentralized society. It sees us as stewards of our resources, inner and outer. It says that we are not victims, not pawns, not limited by conditions and conditioning.*[2]

Back in 1987, the *New Age Journal* conducted a reader survey in which people were invited to give their definitions of the coming new age. One person described it as 'ultimately a vision of a world transformed, a heaven on earth, a society in which the problems of today are overcome and a new existence emerges'. Another wrote of 'moving into an era that emphasizes self-discovery, spiritual growth, and enlightenment'.[3] The agenda is still the same today, though if anything it has become more self-consciously spiritual.

Not totally unrelated to the astrological speculation is the fact that we are now at the start of a new millennium. Just as the year 1000 witnessed an intensifying of eschatological speculation, so a similar phenomenon has surfaced again. People who would not be attracted by the esoteric aspects of the New Age vision are still drawn to a movement that seems to correspond to their own hope that a new millennium will provide the opportunity for a fresh start.

This idea first came to popular attention back in the 1960s, with the rock musical *Hair* and its popular theme song, 'This is the Age of Aquarius', which defined it as 'the age of the mind's true liberation'. But it was not until the late 1980s that the New Age movement became widely known as a way in which people could prepare themselves for this coming age of enlightenment and personal fulfilment. Like any cultural movement, it did not come from nowhere, and many of its elements had been around for a long time before that. As long ago as 1907 a book called *The Aquarian Gospel of Jesus Christ* had promoted a similar idea. But public awareness has grown noticeably in the last decade or so. Academics like Marilyn Ferguson and Hollywood stars like Shirley Maclaine have had enormous influence through their books and public pronouncements on the subject. At the same time, management consultants have spread the New Age message across the corporate world of business executives. And many who would never have thought of themselves as religious, let alone mystics, have found themselves coming into contact with its exponents through their involvement in the environmental movement, especially that subsection of it which specializes in 'deep ecology'. When the UK Green Party held its first annual conference in 1989, journalists and political commentators were spellbound as they watched delegates begin each day with an act of 'attunement' to Gaia. Today, the presence of this kind of spirituality is taken for granted in British politics. The Natural Law Party has contested national elections throughout the 1990s, though its claim that the practice of yogic flying will solve the world's problems has yet to gain sufficient support to win a parliamentary seat.

One of the things that holds together all these apparently contrasting strands is the shared vision of the arrival of a new age of enlightenment and harmony. Like their Christian equivalents, the New Age apocalyptists hedge their bets when trying to determine an exact time for the onset of this new age. According to some, it has already arrived, though most predict that it will dawn some time between now and about the middle of the twenty-first century, perhaps heralded by the arrival of a messiah figure, Maitreya. Much contemporary thinking is undoubtedly dominated by a feeling that things cannot continue as they are for much longer, and that if the new millennium truly is to be a time when we can break free from the mistakes of the past, many things will have to change – not least the attitudes and outlook of people and institutions. A paradigm shift will have to take place, in which we look at ourselves and our world in a holistic way rather than through the fragmentation that has produced so much misery. This paradigm shift will open people's minds to new possibilities, and lead to a changed outlook, that breaks away from the bad habits of the past and makes an open-ended commitment to discovering new ways for the future. It will be a post-colonial worldview, that recognizes the basic injustices and oppressions created, whether deliberately or not, by modern Western culture, and that enables people to build on the insights of modern scientific knowledge, while exploring other less rational dimensions of existence and experience. Part of this will be a fresh awareness of and appreciation for the spiritual insights of non-Western people, together with a move away from rationalist materialism towards an appreciation for a more mystical world of the spirit, in which people can actually experience a new way of life for themselves. As British aristocrat Sir George Trevelyan has put it: 'We are approaching a crucial turning point … Much may have to fall away in our present social structures, but a new society may then emerge in which the unifying spiritual impulse is genuinely at work.'[4]

It is in this context that anything offering the possibility of a change in human outlook is being seized upon with great enthusiasm. Elements from Eastern mysticism combine with modern psychoanalysis, meditation techniques and 'alternative' medical therapies to produce a complex maze of pathways to personal fulfilment and wholeness. Alongside this interest in personal transformation, the insights of political movements that are pressing for social change can also be incorporated – hence the popularity among New Agers of well-known organizations like Amnesty International, Greenpeace or Friends of the Earth, as well as lesser-known movements such as Pulse of the Planet or the Peace Navy. For the most part, these organizations would not describe themselves as 'New Age'. Some of them have been around for a long time, and have no possible connection at all with New Age ideas. But in the New Age networks, everything operates by association. Anything and everything that has potential for promoting a change of thinking among the world's people will be sucked up and utilized, and there is no apparent need to systematize it or to make it all hang together. The only consideration that determines a thing's value – whether it be a large organization or a personal spiritual technique – will be its usefulness in promoting transformation, on either a personal or a global, cosmic scale. How such a transformation will be brought about is still uncertain. As William Irwin Thomson says in his book *From Nation to Emancipation*: 'Whether the movement from one world system to another will involve stumbling or total collapse may very well depend on the success or failure of the new age movement.'[5]

Faced with such uncertainty, some New Agers have set up separate communities to ensure their own safety through the coming world trauma. In remote regions of the USA, thousands of members of the New Age Church Universal and Triumphant have invested heavily in underground bunkers which will allegedly provide security for them when doomsday comes. The leader of this particular group, Elizabeth Clare Prophet, has predicted several times that the end would arrive, but on each occasion so far the Ascended Masters who gave her the information have changed their minds, reputedly as a result of the 'decreeing' (rapid chanting) of the group's members. One of the most highly publicized events designed to enhance spiritual awareness was the universal 'Harmonic Convergence' on 16–17 August 1987, when New

Agers gathered at sacred sites all over the world, from England's Stonehenge to California's Mount Shasta, the Great Pyramid of Cheops in Egypt and the top of the Andes in Peru. The purpose was to 'synchronize the Earth with the rest of the galaxy', and the organizer, Jose Arguelles, announced that as a result of the spiritual energies of those who took part, 'great, unprecedented outpourings of extraterrestrial intelligence ... will be clearly received'. Basing his calculations on various Mayan and Aztec astrological predictions, Arguelles – who holds a Ph.D. from Chicago University – envisaged this great global festival of shamanic chanting, drumming and meditation as the point at which the world's values would begin to change. He predicted that the whole process would end by 1992, when 'the phase shift transiting civilization from a military state of terror to a de-industrialized, decentralized, post-military planetary society will be complete at least in its foundations'.[6]

The pre-event publicity declared that 'The call is out for 144,000 Rainbow Humans to gather at sacred sites all over the earth for the two days from sunrise August 16th to sunrise August 18th', and promised that 'Energy will flow through the linked network of sacred sites ... as we learn to become co-creators and friends with God.' Unfortunately, it did not quite work out that way: only 20,000 people got involved, and many of them were disappointed by the outcome. As a result, today's New Agers are likely to be somewhat more cautious in their claims and predictions. But there are still many thousands of spiritual pilgrims who regularly congregate at sacred sites around the world with the same mood of expectancy. In addition, there are very many more who accept that, while the Age of Aquarius may not yet have dawned, its arrival is certain, and spiritually aware individuals will tune in to its values so as to be ready when the day comes. Most New Age therapies are believed to provide ways of achieving this state of spiritual readiness, usually by inducing altered or new-dimensional levels of consciousness.

A Failed Cultural Vision

To understand the origins of all this, a brief (and necessarily very incomplete) overview of the last five hundred years of Western history and culture will help to set the scene. For it is no coincidence that the New Age movement emerged in the run-up to the start of a new millennium after a period of immense change in world civilization. Change is nothing new: it has been a way of life throughout the world for half a millennium and more. Beginning with the great European explorers in the fourteenth and fifteenth centuries, there has been a non-stop explosion of knowledge that has radically affected the way we all live and think. Prior to the beginning of the process of globalization, life was a pretty simple affair, both for the Europeans who started it and for those in other countries who have found their own cultures gradually swamped by Eurocentric values. Life was not particularly easy, for in Europe itself life expectancy was low, the chance of economic advancement was non-existent for most, and merely to exist was an uphill struggle. But in spite of such hardship, people had a simple view by which to make sense of it all. The earth was a flat disc. Underneath was the world of the dead. Up aloft was heaven. Civilization was mostly concentrated around the shores of the Mediterranean Sea. Global confrontation was generally limited to petty skirmishes between local tyrants.

So long as God was up in his heaven (and, like other European leaders, was indubitably male), all was well. Keeping God there was merely a matter of doing the right things in the right places at the right times. Religion permeated the whole of life. For peasant farmers, sowing seeds and other agricultural operations had religious overtones. For politicians, national strategies were invariably bound up with religious observance. Though there were no doubt many discontinuities and tensions in such a life, everyone shared more or less the same worldview and lived with the same set of settled expectations.

But such a world could not last for ever. Nor did it. First came the explorers. People in the European heartland had known for a long time of the existence of other countries seemingly more esoteric and mystical than their own. In particular, the Bible lands at the eastern end of the Mediterranean had always been places of pilgrimage for those who could afford to go – and some of the bravest European warriors had lost their lives in futile battles for possession of these places. But the possibility of travel to such foreign parts soon inspired others with dreams of lands even more remote. As Spanish and Portuguese navigators looked over the Atlantic Ocean towards the setting sun, they wondered what they might find beyond the horizon. It was only a matter of time before they determined to test the validity of their theories by embarking on long and dangerous ocean crossings. Many did not survive. But those who made it back to their homelands carried with them souvenirs of strange and distant places, and told hair-raising tales that only served to inspire others to join this exciting enterprise for themselves. The discovery that Europe was less than half the world came as a great shock to nations who had previously taken it for granted that they *were* the world, though it provided a major impetus to others who, while lacking the skills and opportunity to discover new lands, threw themselves with great energy into the search for new light on other, hitherto unknown aspects of the world and its workings. If so much of the world was yet to be discovered, how could we be certain about anything? Was the earth actually a flat disc? Was it really the centre of the universe? And if not, what was the truth about it all? Are humans different from animals? And if we know the answers to all these questions, do we need belief in a God who is wiser than ourselves in order to make sense of it all?

It was only a matter of time before there began to emerge answers so startling that leading European thinkers realized they were not just engaged in a search for personal enlightenment: they were caught up in a movement so vast and exciting that they were soon talking of it as *the* Enlightenment. The changes in human knowledge and understanding that took place at this time were so far-reaching that it seemed as if all that had gone before was total darkness compared with the great light that was now dawning. People began to see the world through new eyes, and from different perspectives. Nothing would ever be the same again.

New discoveries were made at breathtaking speed. Barriers began to fall in every area of human understanding. The Polish astronomer Nicolaus Copernicus (1473–1543) reformulated our entire understanding of the workings of the universe – and it came to be taken for granted that, contrary to ancient belief, the world was not a flat disc but a round globe. Almost two centuries later, English scientist and mathematician Sir Isaac Newton (1642–1727) lay in an orchard reflecting on why apples always fall down and not up – and thought of the concept of gravity to explain it. Great advances in understanding the physical universe became almost daily occurrences, as scientists explored and articulated 'laws of nature' that would give a coherent explanation to many things that had previously seemed semi-miraculous. In due course others began to develop medical science, with its great potential for not only understanding how the body works, but actually improving its performance and offering enhanced vitality and life expectancy to all. Then hard on the heels of all this progress came the Industrial Revolution, the development of technology and the invention of modern forms of transportation. Inevitably, as new worlds were opened up, the developing self-confidence of the European Enlightenment was spread far beyond its own continent with the consolidation of empires in other parts of the world. And so was born that phenomenon we now call 'Western culture': a total worldview and way of life that would ultimately – for good or ill – leave no part of the world wholly untouched by its influence.

These must have been exciting times in which to live – at least for Europeans, especially the upper classes, and including in particular the intelligentsia of the day. For we should not forget that almost without exception, European explorers were not content until they had ransacked the natural treasures of other cultures, and enslaved their peoples. Those who survived to be traded as slaves were the fortunate ones, for many millions of their compatriots were butchered without mercy, and the social structures of their communities were left in a ruinous state from which continents like Africa are still struggling to recover. Whole races were virtually wiped out, either by the importation of diseases to which they had no natural resistance or (as in the case of Australian aboriginals) because they were considered to be animals, and not human at all. Over a 400-year period, the native American population was reduced from an estimated 7–10 million to just 250,000. Moreover, this kind of oppression was not reserved only for those of different ethnic origins, for it was during this period that the British authorities identified Australia as a suitable dumping ground for the poorer and more oppressed elements of their own population, who could be transported there for misdemeanours as insignificant as stealing a loaf of bread. Towards the end of this period the Highland Clearances in Scotland led to the displacement of entire populations who were in effect forced into exile in newly discovered lands around the world, while similar consequences followed from the Irish Potato Famine.

The social and intellectual elites of Europe seem to have been oblivious to all this. They could see only the great advances that were being made in technological progress, and the consequent philosophical shift that took place in the way they believed the world and its inhabitants could most truly be understood. From their perspective (if not in the view of the underclasses that they had helped to create all around the world), the days when people might turn to superstition, mythology and religion as a means of unravelling life's mysteries were now firmly in the past. In fact, from the perspective of this elitist philosophy, rooted in its own self-importance, these were the very things that had kept people in ignorance for so long. For the source of all these new ideas that catapulted humanity from the medieval world into the modern age was not some esoteric revelation from another plane of existence. It had all come about simply and solely as human beings had thought long and hard about the world and its workings, and had come up with cool, calculated, logical – and therefore 'scientific' – answers. They did not always get it right first time, of course. But even then, the systematic and patient testing of conflicting hypotheses and theories usually won through to the truth in the end. It seemed as if there was nothing that the trained, intelligent human person could not do. There was always at the heart of this vision a self-destroying mechanism, for 'the autonomy of the rational individual' so beloved of Enlightenment-inspired thinkers was always that of the upper-class, educated individual – 'educated', that is, according to the canons of Western knowledge. More or less up until our own time, this has allowed Western intellectuals to marginalize the insights of other cultures (including other classes in their own), whether they be about science, religion, spirituality or human nature. Arguably one of the contributory factors to the amazing rise of the New Age has been the realization that this self-opinionated dismissal of anything that seems to be non-rational is not only indefensible, but has actually engendered a disregard for the very values that might now help us to chart a new way forward, and therefore has been a major contributor (at least by default) to the chaos in which Western culture now finds itself.

The most notable achievement of this kind of scientific rationalism probably came when, in due course, even the barriers of the physical world itself were broken, and a human being was sent into space. Soviet cosmonaut Yuri Gagarin returned from his historic space flight in 1961, and triumphantly declared that he had seen no sign of God up there, a statement that many people felt was a final epitaph for the possibility of any kind of religious worldview. Given the time, money and expertise, nothing now seemed beyond the grasp of human ingenuity. When scientists could give precise answers to all the questions, who would still need God as a means of explaining things? The answer seemed obvious: no one. In so far as religion would survive in the modern world, it could only ever be a prop for people who in various ways were considered intellectually substandard and psychologically inadequate.

That is how it all seemed forty years ago. Religion – especially traditional Christianity – had every appearance of being in a state of terminal decline. As long ago as 1883 the German philosopher Friedrich Nietzsche had declared that 'God is dead', and by the mid-sixties of the twentieth century there were even Christian theologians ready to agree with him. The traditional idea of God had, of course, been under threat for quite some time, not only from unchristian rationalist thinkers, but also from Christians who themselves tried to redefine their faith by reference to rationalist categories.

Back in the eighteenth century, earnest believers had sought to preserve the Bible from falling into the hands of rationalist historians who saw it not as a special book at all, but as a historical document just like any other of its times. One of the leading Christians in this debate was the great German theologian, Friedrich Schleiermacher (1768–1834). Fired by a genuine desire to protect religious belief from the onslaughts of people whom he regarded as infidels and atheists, he came up with a definition of belief that would declare it to be beyond the reach of reason altogether. The essence of true faith, he claimed, was quite different from things like behaviour or science. Religion was all about pure feeling – and, by definition, that could never be subjected to thoroughgoing intellectual analysis. That being the case, it would not really matter what rationalist historians made of the Bible and other apparently tangible manifestations of faith, for they could never get to the heart of the matter by that route.

Schleiermacher's distinction between the world of science and reason and the world of religion was so widely accepted by Christians that he came to be known as 'the father of modern theology'. It led to what many outside the churches regarded as a kind of intellectual schizophrenia on the part of those still in them. For it meant that Christian scholars could approach the historical and literary aspects of Christianity in a thoroughly rationalistic way, while still preserving some sort of belief in God – a God, however, who could never be understood by reference to the very standards and values which they themselves both believed in and practised! The church, along with other cultural institutions in the West, found itself willingly swallowed up by the new, self-confident, all-pervading worldview dominated by the progress of science, reason, technology and materialism, and in the process it implicitly accepted that spirituality (if it had any relevance to life at all) was effectively a personal matter, to be pursued by those still interested in it only in their own private lives. As a consequence, when (to take just one example) great social and moral issues demanded an answer, the church too often found itself with nothing to say, for it had already concluded that Christianity is not about public life, but about personal preferences. Some of the greatest injustices of the twentieth century – most notably the Holocaust – went largely unchallenged by the church.

Looking back, we can see many ironies in the course taken by Western theology during this period. It has always surprised me that in the 1930s, leading theologians like Rudolf Bultmann were 'demythologizing' Christianity in order to make it more acceptable to a mechanistic worldview at the very moment when science was already in the process of remythologizing the world, inspired by the work of Albert Einstein! At a time when people in the wider culture were becoming ever more sensitive to the need for a holistic way of being that would bring together and integrate different aspects of the human personality not only with one another but with the wider natural environment, the church for the most part stuck to its exclusively rational understanding of the nature of belief, thereby perpetuating not only a privatized notion of faith but also sending out the (often unspoken) message that Christianity is concerned only with what people think, and not with how they feel. In the process, it successfully distanced itself even further from the needs of a generation that was becoming increasingly dominated by the need for emotional healing of damaged relationships and disturbed personalities. As Ian Wray has succinctly put it, Christianity came to be about

> *dwelling intellectually, upon the dogma, with a consequent lack of therapeutic, by which I mean the lack of any real body of ideas and practices to help people change. The near total absence of practical aids to human psychological and spiritual growth within Christianity left a vacuum which [the New Age] had to fill, based upon principles which it had to discover for itself.*[7]

We shall return in more detail to the implications of all this in our final chapter. Here it is sufficient to observe that factors such as these go a considerable way towards explaining why the Western church is in such bad shape today, and why many spiritual searchers take it for granted that, if there is an answer to our present predicament, the last place it will be found is within the Christian church. For even as Yuri Gagarin circled the earth with his confident message of technology come of age, storm clouds were gathering which would in the following thirty years radically change the contours of much of the Western cultural landscape. Looking back, we can now see that the message of the 'death of God' theologians of the sixties was more of an epitaph for Western Enlightenment culture than it was for religion *per se*. Indeed, ever since then religious belief in the broadest sense has been experiencing a vigorous revival. Clayton Carlson has been an interested observer of the cultural scene throughout his life. When I spoke with him, he was senior vice-president of one of America's largest publishing houses, and had reached that position largely as a result of his skill for anticipating cultural trends before they happened, and ensuring that the right books would be written and available at the right time. Sitting in his office in a trendy part of San Francisco's waterfront area, he reflected on his own experience. A quarter of a century before, as a young man, he had begun his career in New York. Most people moving to the big cities of the east coast at that time came from traditional backgrounds in small towns, where going to church was one of the ways of showing they were good solid citizens. But to make progress in the 'high culture' of Manhattan, they generally repressed all that, because it was widely regarded as irrelevant. 'If you were interested in religious things,' commented Carlson, 'it was somehow sub-cultural certainly a symbol of psychological weakness. But today? That has gone. Absolutely gone. If anything, it is *avant garde* to be religious. Overall in the culture now, the openness to the spirit is just enormous.' As a publisher, he should know, for Christian publications now account for more than a third of all US commercial book sales, while New Age books are the fastest growing sector of the market throughout the world.

One does not need to visit California to see the truth of that, but it is certainly one of the places that leads where others only follow. What was happening there ten years ago is now commonplace in Britain and Australia, while California has moved on. The whole place is just buzzing with mystical awareness – coupled with a serious spiritual search for new answers to the human predicament. Why else would leading figures from many walks of life put their reputations on the line by openly publicizing their experiences of the spirit world? Relaxing in his Walnut Creek home,

Ron Valle, transpersonal psychologist and former professor at Orinda's John F. Kennedy University, put it to me this way: 'I think there's a basic frustration in all of us. The mystery of God, the mystery of awe has been taken away – at least for the lay person – by science. There's no room in our culture for the kind of experience we all long for. We're starving spiritually.' In that final sentence he encapsulated what today's new spiritual search is all about. Despite all the science, all the technology, all the institutions and expertise, people still have a gap in their lives. As they look at their everyday lifestyles – shopping, work, education, recreation, relationships – many ask what the purpose of it all might be. Though it is not easy to articulate, there is a widespread feeling that the quality of life is getting worse all the time, and that the scientific, technological and social change of the last two hundred years is getting us nowhere. Somewhere along the line, some fundamental human and spiritual values have been lost. Millions of people, in all walks of life and from all social classes, sense an increased yearning for something spiritual, and ever-increasing numbers of thinking people are reaching the conclusion that the world is in such a mess precisely because we have lost touch with spiritual meaning. Faced with a world that seems to be spinning out of control, with average temperatures rising all around the globe as the planet itself chokes to death on industrial pollution, more people than ever before are searching for something sacred, and are desperate to find spiritual satisfaction in a consumerist world.

Regaining Paradise Lost

How and why has this happened? Simple questions rarely have straightforward answers, and this one is no exception. But we can say one thing without hesitation. The New Age movement is a response to the acknowledged failure of the scientific and materialist worldview to deliver the goods. The great Enlightenment vision of a better world for everyone has simply not materialized. Not only has the fundamental human predicament not improved, but as the twentieth century progressed things actually got worse. What is more, the increasing pace of change and the accompanying difficulties of keeping up with it are hitting people everywhere – in the workplace and the family, as well as on the global and international scene. Things are happening today that, quite simply, have never happened before in the whole of time. For instance, the speed at which we can now travel and communicate has increased more in this generation than in every other generation there has ever been! That is a simple example. But it is symptomatic of what is now taking place at every level of human existence. Who in the early 1980s would have believed that by the end of the decade Communism could have collapsed so totally in Eastern Europe – and done so almost literally overnight? Or that in the light of what happened subsequently in many of these lands, what US President Ronald Reagan once called 'the evil empire' now looks like a regime of unparalleled safety and security, for the West at least? Change is nothing new, but in previous generations things tended to change slowly, which meant people would adapt quite easily as part of a naturally evolving process. The faster the pace of change, the more difficult it is to handle, and the solutions to today's problems are likely to be redundant long before they can be implemented. The world is moving on all the time, which means we are likely to fall further and further behind in coping with things. No wonder that these increasing pressures are demanding a reappraisal of some of the most basic questions of all. Matters that our grandparents thought had been settled for all time are now up for debate again – questions about the world and its systems, about life and its meaning, about people and their relationships, about values and religion. In general, we are becoming less and less satisfied with the traditional answers of Western culture.

Science and technology have produced many benefits, which it would be impossible – and foolish – to deny. Modern medical science must surely have improved the lifestyle of most of us, and the development of efficient world-wide transportation systems has done much to open our eyes to the global dimensions of our own lives. But the course of progress has not run smoothly. A hundred years ago, it was confidently believed that as evolution progressed the human race must be improving all the time. It is impossible to believe that any more. For the senseless carnage of the First World War, followed by the genocide of the Holocaust, were not isolated shameful episodes. On the contrary, they turned out to be typical of international relationships throughout the twentieth century, which has seen more bloody conflicts than any other comparable period in the whole of history. Whatever the politicians claim, the world is still a brutal place for most of its people. When I was a child, nuclear power was in its infancy, and I well remember the propaganda informing us that science held the promise of a better future for the world, and technology would bring us all incredible happiness. Who would believe that today?

We need to be fair, of course, and recognize that most of the advances there have been did not need to lead to the consequences we now see. Who could have foreseen that so many scientific discoveries would be used to develop ever more terrifying ways of annihilating people? Who could have imagined that improving standards of health care, leading to longer life expectancy and falling rates of infant mortality, would enable the world's population to increase to the point where many nations are constantly balanced on a knife-edge between survival and extinction? Who could have predicted that the efficient use of fertilizers and pesticides to produce more food for this expanding population would lead to the pollution of the world's water, one of the most precious resources of all? How could anyone have guessed that the development of modern transportation systems, and the fuels used to operate them, would lead to the depletion of the ozone layer, with its evident results in unpredictable climatic change?

In addition to the insecurities generated by these concerns, an enormous number of people have, for one reason or another, lost faith in their institutions, and conclude that the remaining structures are concerned mainly for their own survival and welfare as institutions. Mistrust and cynicism are the order of the day. At one time medics, with their strict Hippocratic oath and commitment to other people's welfare, were highly regarded as the least corruptible profession of all. Today they are widely viewed with suspicion as people with more interest in patient hours and covering their overheads than in the health and welfare of those whom they treat. Even those patients who are not quite so cynical still find themselves drawn to alternative therapies and holistic health techniques, simply because the professional medic no longer has enough time to deal adequately with the needs of every single patient.

Establishment religion fares no better. The churches have always had an uneasy relationship with Enlightenment values, but they have generally adopted them by default as their own dominant worldview, and are now in the process of suffering the consequences. As a result, many who are on the fringes of organized religion have come to believe that whatever spiritual reality there once was has been siphoned off or suppressed in the interests of the ecclesiastical establishment, and that the professional clergy are so concerned with keeping the machinery going and maintaining their own vested interests in power and position that they too have lost touch with any kind of movement of the spirit. There is a widespread feeling that if the mystical side of religion is to be rediscovered, it will not be in the mainstream establishment, but on the fringes – whether in individualistic forms of Christianity or in the transformational therapies of the New Age movement. Many people would resonate with the claim of the New Age Universal 'Christianity without Religion' movement, based in the

Canary Islands, when its publicity warns: 'You owe it to your God to stay away from organized institutionalized man-made religion,' and then continues, 'Empty prayer in empty churches is noise,' urging readers, 'You can become a living church without religion, so act now – serve God, not man!'

Whether all this is a wholly accurate analysis of Western culture is not our concern just now. The fact is that enough people believe it for it to have a significant impact. It seems that we have not been able to change or improve the world even by our own best efforts. The Enlightenment dream has turned into a nightmare. But the dream will not go away. People still aspire to a better life, in which we can live in harmony with one another, at peace with our planet and in tune with ourselves. The longing for a 'new age' is deeply-rooted in the human heart, and if traditional Western materialist routes to personal fulfilment and transformation are blocked, then we must have been looking in the wrong direction.

It is a basic assumption of most New Agers that after the Enlightenment some genuine spiritual values and insights got lost. Because of the dominance of rationalism and reasonableness, the current establishment options are therefore pale remnants of the spiritual fire that started them all – and to recover a sense of our own destiny and purpose, we need to get back to the fire again. In the effort to do so, mystical traditions of the past such as Gnosticism or the Qabbalah rub shoulders with the speculations of science fiction, much of which now has a mystical and spiritual character. In the search for ultimate answers, people will as readily look to traditional shamans as to extra-terrestrial visitors from other planets. Things that were being dismissed as worthless superstitions a generation ago are now projected on to the centre stage as the key to the meaning of life's mysteries, as various ancient traditions are re-examined for possible contact with some kind of metaphysical wisdom. The public has an insatiable appetite for mythical traditions of all kinds, and almost overnight, ancient and long-forgotten mysteries have become the way to get things straight.

Many reactionary movements operate in this way, assuming that the stranger a thing is, the more authentic it is likely to be. It is therefore no surprise that it is often taken for granted that truth is some kind of mystical, secret thing which our cultural institutions have buried in order to preserve their own vested interests. We can see this quite clearly in the way so many people eagerly embrace 'alternative' practices in areas like medicine, health and education, as well as in the more narrowly defined religious realm. As a result, anything that seems to be coming from another place – preferably ancient and non-Western – has a running start. Clayton Carlson observed: 'When I started being interested in this, the major issue was credulity. People had difficulty in believing. Now the problem is incredulity – people will in reaction believe anything.' But even that is, according to some, perfectly 'reasonable'. For it is now being claimed that cutting-edge science, with notions such as uncertainty or chaos, can justify a more intuitive approach to truth. Put simply, it was the old science of people like Newton that led us into a blind alley, with its insistence on unchangeable 'laws of nature' and its assumption that things work on a cause-and-effect basis like well-oiled machinery. But the new science, developed largely after Einstein, has opened up new possibilities. Even matter itself may not be as solid as it seems, but could just be one manifestation of the energy that runs through everything in the universe. Scientists who are also New Agers are not slow to jump to that conclusion, and readily identify the dynamic viewpoint of modern physics with the age-old beliefs of (especially) religions like Hinduism or Buddhism, that 'God', people and the earth itself are all fundamentally different aspects of the one cosmic reality.

In his best-selling book, *The Turning Point*, Fritjof Capra, Professor of Physics at the University of California in Berkeley, observes:

The new concepts in physics have brought about a profound change in our world view; from the mechanistic conception of Descartes and Newton to a holistic or ecological view, a view which I have found to be similar to the views of mystics of all ages and traditions.[8]

Who are the New Agers?

Dissatisfaction with the establishment is nothing new in the recent history of the West. Back in the 1960s, such feelings surfaced through radical student movements and the whole hippie phenomenon. There are some connections between that and the New Age, but its origins should not be traced exclusively to those groups. The protesters of the sixties were almost entirely young people, whereas today's New Age movement cuts across all age groups. Moreover, the sixties protests were often bound up with the use of drugs and other anti-establishment lifestyles, whereas today's New Agers are more likely to be found living quietly in suburbia, with the same trappings of prosperity and success as everyone else. They are mechanics, nurses, engineers, secretaries, police officers, psychologists, teachers – a regular cross-section of society.

Of course, many of the people who are living in the suburbs today were the kids of the sixties. During the intervening decades they have been busy raising their families and progressing in their careers, and now they have reached mid-life. Without necessarily turning it into a crisis, this is a natural point at which to take stock of one's achievements, and to determine how to spend the rest of one's life. For many, this is a stage in life when there is more time and opportunity to indulge in visionary idealism. Religion may have been put aside for twenty or thirty years while they got on with the more serious business of making money and creating a comfortable lifestyle. But once those goals have been achieved, quite a few try to rediscover their spiritual roots, or start for the first time to read serious psychological material, or delve into the great classics of ancient literature and philosophy.

Traditionally, the religious roots that such people went to would have been the Christian church. In the past, they frequently turned to it at times of crisis or uncertainty. When America was changing from an agricultural to an industrial society in the mid-1700s, the economic transformation was accompanied by what has been called the Great Religious Awakening. Nearer to our own time, in the 1950s, following the Second World War, people in America (though not generally in Britain) went back to church in a big way. But those who grew up in the 1960s have a different outlook on life. For a whole variety of reasons – immigration, greater global awareness, dissatisfaction with Christianity – they are more conscious of the fact that the church is apparently not the only way to find new meaning in life. There is a wide range of options out there just waiting to be explored, most of them a good deal more appealing than what is known about Christianity.

For while Christianity seems to encapsulate all the weaknesses of Western culture, New Age thinking claims to encompass what is good and transform it into something even better. It is not a drug-based counter-culture, but it can easily endorse and build on the experiences of expanded consciousness of those who took LSD back in the sixties, contextualizing them as early experiments in what is now a much larger, more serious search for spiritual meaning. The 'new science' has also been widely applauded within the New Age and eagerly incorporated into its worldview, thereby offering a spiritual basis for living without also rejecting those very aspects of modern technology which have produced the creature comforts we all like to enjoy. The New Age is also the ultimate fulfilment of the great American dream. It may not have actually started in California, but it is not accidental that this has been one of its major recruiting grounds. The United States itself, and the west coast in particular, has always been perceived as the place to make a new start. Free from the inhibitions, weaknesses and failures of the past, the New Age vision presents ever more attractive possibilities for a change and transformation that can encompass every aspect of life – from the acquisition of a new healthy body to the realization of some of the more esoteric elements of American national consciousness. American New Agers often draw attention to the fact that – unlike the European cultural heritage – their whole society has a distinctively mystical foundation. A majority of the leaders of the Wars of Independence were personally connected with mystical traditions – a fact that ordinary citizens are reminded of every day, for not only does the Great Seal declare on its reverse that 'A New Order of the Ages Begins', but the dollar bill still carries on its reverse side symbols drawn from Rosicrucian, Masonic, and Hermetic traditions. Marilyn Ferguson has compared the New Age movement with the foundational events of the US state, describing it as 'the second American revolution', and claiming that

> *American society has at hand most of the factors that could bring about collective transformation: relative freedom, relative tolerance, affluence enough to be disillusioned with affluence, achievements enough to know that something different is needed.*[9]

When set in this context, it is tempting to regard the New Age movement as yet another example of the kind of outmoded drum-beating colonialism that has led us into the present confrontational world situation which New Agers claim to dislike so much. Could it be that the New Age is actually a more subtle form of imperialism for a post-colonial world? Not a political imperialism now, for that would be impractical. But an intellectual imperialism, that claims everyone else thinks the wrong way and must be brought into line in the cause of justice, peace, harmony and wholeness. This is the classic line taken by empire-builders since the very beginning of time, and its resurgence not only within the New Age, but also in postmodernity more generally, has been well highlighted by the Islamic writer Ziauddin Sardar, who comments that

> *when western thought reaches a dead end, it unreservedly turns towards [other cultures] to appropriate and devour [their] thought and continue on its irrational and grotesquely skewed goal ... [which turns out to be] simply a new wave of domination riding on the crest of colonialism and modernity.*[10]

There can be no question that some New Agers fall into that category, and speak freely of bringing about one great world consciousness, in which everyone will be the same. It is doubtful right now whether the New Age as such is sufficiently well organized to deliver anything like that. But the vision of a world so changed that it will present us with genuinely new possibilities will continue, because it appeals to the natural aspirations of human beings, and augments the hopes and ambitions of many at the beginning of a new millennium. Because it is not a structured organization, the various elements which currently find themselves sucked into the New Age orbit will no doubt be rearranged and regrouped many times. Some will fall out, others will come in to take their place. The exact shape of the New Age is constantly changing, and it will not be the same in five years as it is today. But whatever shape it adopts, it will be with us for some time, simply because it reflects so authentically the deepest longings of the human spirit. Secular humanism is now largely a spent force, though it still has its supporters, notably among philosophers and theologians. The traditional Judeo-Christian religion of the Western world has all but collapsed, and though the unprecedented growth of the church throughout other parts of the world has ensured that Christianity is still the largest of all world faiths, it is not yet clear what impact that might have on the emerging global culture. Because of the dominance of Western culture throughout the world, whenever the West suffers from a major crisis of confidence, it is bound to have repercussions elsewhere. The rapid collapse of the Enlightenment vision has created a powerful spiritual vacuum at the centre of our civilization. Whether New Age thinking will rush in to fill it, only time will tell. Whether it deserves to do so, and what the consequences may be, is a question we must now try and answer.

Chapter Three

'Going Within'

Perhaps the best known of all the advocates of New Age spirituality is Hollywood actress Shirley Maclaine. Through her TV interviews, newspaper and magazine articles – and especially the autobiographical book *Out on a Limb*, which formed the basis of the TV mini-series of the same name – she has done more than anyone else to alert ordinary people to the fact that some remarkable things can happen in the course of the search for spiritual meaning in life.

Her own story is typical of many people in the baby boomer generation. She was brought up in a traditional way; God was a natural part of life, and for her family going to church was as normal an activity as going to school or the supermarket. As a child and a teenager, Shirley Maclaine simply took religion for granted and committed herself to what she knew and understood of the teachings of Christianity. But as adolescence gave way to adulthood with all the demands of an independent home and career, she gradually let go of her involvement with Christianity, and in due course drifted away from the church altogether.

Searching for the Spiritual

If this was just the personal story of a famous movie star, it would have been of little interest outside the circles of trendy gossip columnists. But it is also the story of vast multitudes of other people who have been brought up within the church. While the exact details might vary from one case study to another, what followed Shirley Maclaine's drift from Christianity is absolutely typical of huge numbers of today's spiritual searchers. She did not lose her faith in religion in the broadest sense – nor did she find it either possible or desirable to suppress her deep conviction that, if life has any real meaning, the key to it all must be found in the realm of the spiritual and the super-natural. Personal maturity and professional success engendered within her a deeper fascination for, and growing commitment to, the search for some spiritual meaning behind it all. Like many of her generation, she began to wonder if other cultures – especially mystical Eastern religions – might have more to say than her own strict Christian background. Unlike most of her contemporaries, she was rich enough to be able to fly around the world with ease, consulting spiritual guides on several continents, and frequently following in the footsteps of other pop stars and actors to India, Nepal, Tibet and similar exotic destinations. All of this was inter-esting, and occasionally helpful, but she only began to find something that spoke to her when she became personally aware of the existence of a whole spiritual realm that is beyond and above the things we can see, touch and handle in everyday life. As a result of a chance meeting with people who claimed to be receiving messages from spiritual entities in some other world, she found herself inescapably drawn into a systematic and deter-mined effort to test the truth of what she was being told. Her quest eventually took her to the top of the Peruvian Andes, where she had a series of remarkable experiences.

There she was persuaded that by immersing herself in warm mineral springs, she could find the pathway to a renewed spiritual awareness. It sounded unlikely – and she herself was sceptical. But as she put it to the test, the most amazing things began to happen. As a result of the combination of the water, the aroma and various breathing exercises, she found herself disengaging from her body and rising into some higher form of existence. In her own words,

My head felt light. I physically felt a kind of tunnel open in my mind ... I had no arms, no legs, no body, no physical form. I became the space in my mind. I felt myself flow into the space, fill it, and float off, rising out of my body until I began to soar. I was aware that my body remained in the water. I looked down and saw it ... My spirit or mind or soul, or whatever it was, climbed higher into space. Right through the ceiling of the pool house and upward over the twilight river ... wafting higher and higher until I could see the mountains and the landscape below me ... attached to my spirit was a thin, thin silver cord that remained stretched though attached to my body in the pool of water. I wasn't in a dream. No, I was conscious of everything ... it felt like a new dimension of perception, somehow, that had nothing to do with hearing or seeing or smelling or tasting or touching.[1]

The silver cord which she saw ensured that in due course she did return to her body, but this first experience of what she later came to recognize as astral projection left a deep and lasting impression on her. It provided the opportunity to be in touch not only with her own inner self but also with another strange world of expanded consciousness, in a way that would ultimately impart a radically new meaning and direction to her entire life.

Many people have reacted to all this with cynicism and disbelief. They have argued that anyone could induce the same experiences by engaging in regulated breathing exercises while immersed in warm water in an oxygen-starved atmosphere – and that, far from putting a person in touch with some new spiritual world, it is nothing more than psychological manipulation. In his review of the five-hour-long TV movie of this story, John Carman, television critic of the *San Francisco Chronicle*, described it as 'deliriously wacko', and went on to wonder whether Shirley Maclaine was, as he put it, 'out on a limb or just plain off her rocker'.[2]

There is no doubt that New Agers need to address themselves to comments of this sort with more rigour than they sometimes do, and to back up personal experience with something that can be tested by other people. But it would be pointless to deny the profound impact that such experiences are having on the lives of many ordinary people. Shirley Maclaine's story has been broadcast around the world only because she happens to be famous. But there are hundreds of thousands of people (maybe more) whose stories parallel hers – and not a few who claim even more spectacular experiences as they pass from one dimension of consciousness to another.

Not many can afford either the time or the money to travel to distant lands, but local therapy centres have sprung up all over the world, offering the same spiritual adventure at a modest price. Here, 'rebirthing' (as it is often called) can take place in the more domesticated atmosphere of a hot tub or Jacuzzi. Attended by a therapist with experience of such things, and with a water temperature of 50°C and twenty minutes or so of controlled breathing, clients can expect to enter a trance-like state leading to a suspension of sensation in arms and legs, as they float in a watery universe that, it is claimed, will ultimately give new meaning and direction to life. Three sessions is reckoned to be the minimum requirement to produce some lasting change, but many people rebirth like this once a week – not always in a hot tub, for the experience can also be carried out 'dry' (and at lower cost) on a futon mattress. But the watery context is generally preferred. It is more intimate, invoking images of actual birth, and is also claimed to accelerate the process of change, leading rapidly from one dimension of consciousness to another in an almost infinite variety of personal spiritual adventures that can impact every area of life. An experienced San Francisco rebirther described it to me as

> a course designed to help you resolve issues on your true work, money and authority figures, while aligning with universal principles ... Rebirthing is the process of getting to know and love your Self. It has to do with freeing your breath, choosing your thoughts, expressing your feelings and healing your body. In essence, it is spiritual purification.

The sharing of personal stories plays a large part in New Age spirituality. An experience-based story can never be either right or wrong: it is simply an account of what has taken place, and its value to the person who tells it is neither diminished nor enhanced by the responses and reactions of other people. This is one of the aspects of the New Age that others often find most puzzling and frustrating. They want to know what New Agers actually believe, and the kind of answer they are looking for would be a systematic statement of beliefs. That is one of the things that most New Age devotees are not going to supply – certainly not if 'belief' is defined in a way in which facts and truth claims are of fundamental importance. For most people in the New Age utilize elements from many different religious traditions, not for their inherent 'truth' so much as for their perceived practical usefulness. Wrestling with the meaning of her own spiritual experience, Shirley Maclaine comments, 'the thing is, it all seems to be about feeling, not thinking'.[3] The same sentiment was expressed by another New Ager who told me that 'half our mistakes in life arise from feeling where we ought to think, and thinking where we ought to feel'.

Western culture has always placed a great deal more emphasis on rational thought than on our feelings and emotions. The great Enlightenment thinkers laid so much stress on the importance of human reason and the supremacy of intellectual brain-power, that they almost reached the point where it was denied that 'truth' could possibly mean anything other than the knowledge of facts. In his speech on 8 August 1968 in which he accepted nomination for the US presidency, Richard Nixon pledged his administration to 'begin by committing ourselves to the truth, to see it like it is and to tell it like it is, to find the truth, to speak the truth and live with the truth. That's what we'll do.' Our whole educational system instils in us the conviction that truth is 'to see it like it is'. It has to do with facts that can be proved rationally by some sort of logical analysis. Therefore beliefs – especially those about the sort of absolutes that religions deal in – must also be related to facts of this same intellectual kind before they can be taken seriously. No doubt that explains why, in the Christian tradition, 'belief' has often found its most perfect expression when people give their formal assent to a set of doctrinal or theological propositions. Even to this day, there are many churches around the world in which a mentally handicapped person cannot become a full member, precisely because being a Christian is understood as requiring a certain level of intellectual acceptance of truths and abstract principles. There are many more which exclude children from full membership on the basis that, until they have reached a certain stage of mental development, they are unlikely to be able either to understand or to commit themselves to religious belief.

It is hardly surprising, then, that many New Agers – inspired by recent brain and mind research – have come to the conclusion that most Westerners are suffering from 'metaphysical amnesia', a condition in which we are rendered incapable of seeing beyond the rational and the reasonable.[4] As a result, they claim, our potential for spiritual fulfilment has been seriously eroded. We have been conditioned to operate through only one half of our brain – the left half, which does the thinking – while the right half, which majors on feeling and perception, has been left undeveloped and immobilized. Many ordinary people would tend to agree with this – even if they take it no further than ensuring they answer the telephone with their left ear when discussing business, while reserving their right ear for affairs of the heart. There is, of course, some truth in it all, overlaid with a thick layer of superstition and wishful thinking. For while it is generally the case that the two sides of the brain control different activities, in people who suffer brain damage the unimpaired hemisphere can take over functions normally performed by the other side. So it is debatable whether our 'metaphysical amnesia' (if, indeed, we suffer from it) is physiologically related to the structure of our brains. We also cannot escape the fact that, though New Agers complain about the one-sided thinking that Western culture promotes, their own understanding of consciousness is itself ultimately reductionist and rationalist. It is inconsistent to contend that anything that can be intuitively verified through the right brain is OK, while logical verification through the left brain is somehow suspect. Whatever else it may be, this kind of reasoning is certainly no more holistic than the inadequate system it is supposed to replace. At the same time, the general points that New Agers are making, though exaggerated, can hardly be denied.

In reality, we all know that rational understanding is only half the story. Our everyday relationships with other people tell us that there is a lot more to life than that. For in that realm, 'belief' has more to do with personal commitment and open communication than with the mere acceptance of facts. If my belief in my wife consisted only of the knowledge of rationally verifiable data such as her birth date, her size, her hair colour, and so on, then we would have a very strange understanding of each other. A relationship cannot proceed very far before emotions and feelings come into the picture – even that supremely non-rational notion we call 'love'.

By contrast, in the mainstream Christian tradition, 'knowing God' has for the most part meant knowing things about God, and quite often pretty abstruse and esoteric things, at that. Belief in God has majored on 'facts' about God, rather than direct personal experience of God's presence. It was once said of the nineteenth-century English churchman, Cardinal John Henry Newman (1801–90), that he believed in God, but he did not trust God. Shirley Maclaine puts it even more succinctly in her report of a conversation with 'John', a channelled spirit entity, who comments: 'Your religions teach religion – not spirituality.'[5] It is the search for spirituality – a mystical essence of personal, direct encounter with 'God' – that is at the heart of much of the New Age movement. In this quest, it is inevitable that hands-on experience is going to be far more important than mere intellectual belief.

Some Common Themes

Having said all that, when New Agers claim they have no beliefs as such, that is not quite the full story. The conviction that subjective experience is more important than objective fact is itself a belief, which may or may not be true. Beyond that, there are also other basic assumptions that look suspiciously like a belief system. In seeking to identify some core to the New Age philosophy, Marilyn Ferguson observes that 'the mystical experience of wholeness encompasses all separation', and explains this by adding that 'This wholeness encompasses self, others, ideas ... You are joined to a great Self ... And because that Self is inclusive, you are joined to all others.'[6]

This appears to be a claim that there is a 'life force', 'energy field' or 'consciousness' that animates the whole of existence. It is found in people and animals, but it also runs through every part of the natural world – grass, trees, mountains, stones, stars, galaxies, and much more besides. They are all bound together into one great system by this energy force that is common to them all. In fact, this energy field is the only ultimate reality there is, which means that finding true meaning and fulfilment in life is a matter of recognizing and accepting one's place in the great cosmic scheme of things.

This point of view is more widely held in the West today than most people realize. The average person in the street may not express it in this kind of jargon, but we have become so accustomed to picking it up from the media that we hardly notice it any more. When *Star Wars* became the first of a long series of Hollywood blockbusters based on the discovery of spiritual forces, conventional greetings like 'Good morning' or 'Good afternoon' were replaced almost overnight by cosmic statements such as 'May the Force be with you'. Many other box office successes have been dominated by similar themes. Indiana Jones gained his reputation by searching for all sorts of magical and spiritual keys to the meaning of life and the cosmos, while many other popular movies have explored similar themes (e.g. *ET, Gremlins, The Exorcist, The X-Files*, to mention only a few). All these, and many others, are based on the assumption of the likely existence of extra-terrestrial life forms, sometimes benevolent and sometimes not. Even the *Superman* series depicts a hero from another world not only entering our own, but through his superior ancient wisdom (and Kryptonite crystals) actually putting right many of the wrongs and injustices that concern us all so deeply.

Such themes are so pervasive in the entertainment industry that film critics have been forced to sharpen up their religious knowledge and spiritual awareness, in order to analyse the messages coming from modern Hollywood.[7] Whether these seemingly spiritual messages are deliberately intended by the directors need not concern us here, though Steven Spielberg has more than once

denied that there is any religion in his films at all. Movies are
one of the key indicators of the nature of our culture, and there
is no denying that, insofar as they mirror the spiritual assumptions
of the day, they consistently present an understanding of 'God'
as a symbol for the whole cosmic process, rather than as the personal being found in the inherited Judeo-Christian worldview.
Contrasting the old 'Machine Age God' of the Age of Pisces with
the new 'Systems Age God' of the Age of Aquarius, internationally
acclaimed management consultant Russell Ackoff encapsulates the
essence of this contemporary view when he says that this new-style
God 'cannot be individualised or personified, and cannot be
thought of as the creator ... In this holistic view of things man is
taken as a part of God just as his heart is taken as a part of man.'[8]

Spiritual psychologist Scott Peck, who is much respected in
many Christian circles, says pretty much the same thing: 'If you
desire wisdom greater than your own, you can find it inside you ...
To put it plainly, our unconscious is God ... It is for the individual
to become totally, wholly God.'[9]

Religious Roots

This view has some obvious antecedents in the world of traditional
religion. Anyone who is familiar with the religious thought of
India will recognize here certain similarities with classical Hinduism. The idea that ultimate reality ('God', if you like) consists of
a kind of cosmic essence, present in all things, is very similar to the
concept of *Brahman*, the universal Reality which was prior to all
other existence. The insistence on personal experience as a thing of
greater authority than holy books or theological 'beliefs' also has
its parallel in the *Gita*, which states, 'As is a pool of water in a place
flooded with water, so are all the *Vedas* [traditional Hindu scrip-
tures] to a person who has attained Enlightenment.'[10]

But the New Age viewpoint is not merely a repetition of traditional Hinduism. It is a common trend among New Agers to take

something that appeals to them, and modify it by combination with other things that also appeal to them, so as to create something new in the synthesis. In this case, parts of a Hindu worldview rub shoulders with bits of Western thinking in ways that traditional Hindus would think were incompatible with one another. For in the East, *Atman* (the individual self) *is* Brahman. As soon as you say that, individual people lose their distinctive identity – something that has little appeal for the 'me generation' which has largely produced the New Age. But in a system that has no place for logical thinking, and is organized purely on the basis of what is useful – what feels right – that is no problem. One can simply combine Western individualism with Eastern mysticism, and give it a new twist. As one New Ager expressed it, 'Sure, all things are divine – especially me!' While another put it to me this way: 'The individual drop never goes into the cosmic bucket. What happens is that the whole bucket gets absorbed into the drop. That makes me a very powerful individual.'

Another difference can be found in the fact that Hinduism is essentially world-denying, seeing salvation in terms of escape from attachment to this material world, whereas New Age people tend to be world-affirming. There are exceptions, but for the most part they have no desire to reject the world – they would rather enjoy it, and change it. This way, one can have the best of everything. This pick-and-mix approach to traditional world religions is typical of how the New Age deals with other people's spirituality. It raises many questions about the purpose and inner coherence of the New Age, not least in relation to the nature of its ethical stance. For this procedure enables evil to be detached and depersonalized, while still keeping people in the centre of things. It appears that the New Age can offer an open door to personal fulfilment in this world, without demanding that anyone should accept personal responsibility for their actions, either in this world or in some other. Many New Agers would celebrate this freedom from accountability as being one of the great benefits of their approach to life, though others would reject such an interpretation as shallow and morally unacceptable. But most would still defend the principle that it is permissible to take elements from different religious systems and mix them together by arguing that since all religions contain some truth – however obscured and hidden it may be – then the 'wisdom of the ages' will be discerned by combining insights from different traditions. Since organized religion has historically been the cause of some of the world's fiercest conflicts, such a move could actually have desirable moral consequences as harmonization might actually speed up the dawning of that age of peace and mutual acceptance that we all long for.

Pick-and-Mix Spirituality

Many of today's spiritual searchers are eager to take elements from all over the spiritual and metaphysical spectrum and combine them in what can seem an indiscriminate and, at times, incoherent way. For those who start from the assumption that 'all is one' (and, as we noted in the first chapter, not all New Agers do), then it naturally follows that life can find its deepest meaning as people get in tune with this one great cosmic life force. But what is it that separates us from it anyway? A common answer is that our experienced separation from this divine force is the creation only of our own consciousness. In that case, we can be 'saved' by utilizing techniques that will lead to the realignment of consciousness. Instead of remaining on the purely rational level, where our culture has conditioned and trained us to operate, we can move on to the attainment of a higher level of consciousness, which will be a spiritual and metaphysical level. By doing this we will be empowered to relate to the wider cosmos, to find our own inner self, and ultimately, to undergo personal transformation. Inevitably, different people will feel a need for change and self-discovery at different points in their lives, and this helps to explain the bewildering assortment of transformational practices that can all, to one degree or another, be identified as 'New Age'. Some of the techniques currently in vogue are mind-blowing, both in their overall variety and in their individual character. They range from demanding physical (sometimes life-threatening) exercises, to complementary health care, to more traditional spiritual activities like meditation or music, and ultimately shading off into areas dominated by the occult. Fire-walking, colour balancing, 'body-work' in many diverse forms, and even sky-diving and belly-dancing, can all be utilized to promote spiritual development. In their book *The Psychic Side of Sports*, Michael Murphy and Rhea A. White claim that any physical activity can enhance spiritual aware-ness: 'the many reports we have collected show us that sport has enormous power to sweep us beyond the ordinary sense of self to evoke capacities that have generally been regarded as mystical, occult, or religious.'[11]

There is no doubt that sport is one of the key points in life where people now express what previous generations would have regarded as religious sentiments. But it is highly debatable whether that is because of its capacity to induce altered states of consciousness or out-of-body experiences.[12]

Getting in touch with nature – or rather, with the spiritual powers of Gaia, Mother Earth – is also the aim behind the many wilderness quests on which one might embark in search of personal meaning and transformation. In the course of her well-publicized spiritual search, Shirley Maclaine visited the Peruvian Andes, and the mountains played a particular role in her remark-able self-discovery. Mount Shasta in Northern California is another location which is said to be specially close to the spiritual powers of the universe, while the same beneficial effects are some-times claimed for treks into the aboriginal homelands of the Australian outback. Some operators even offer package tours to 'the power centres of the earth' – places where spiritual searchers not only find personal healing as they align themselves with the mother goddess, but can also contribute towards the healing of the earth itself, which has been scarred and impaired by generations of insensitive technological exploitation. In the UK, major stopping places on such an itinerary would include Stonehenge and Glastonbury in England, and Findhorn and Iona in Scotland.

Yoga and other body exercises are other popular methods of self-discovery. The 'Dances of Universal Peace', for example, were first evolved in the United States in 1967 by Samuel Lewis, under the guidance of his own teachers, Ruth St Denis and Sufi Inayat Khan, and they have now spread around the world. According to the publicity blurb of one group,

> *The Dances of Universal Peace are an art of movement and sound with feeling that can allow one to move in a new way, to feel unity within and without. The energy created in the circle can fuel life and work on many levels.*

One does not need to be a dancer in order to take part in such movement – 'only a desire to move with devotion and rhythm dedicating oneself to experiencing joy and peace for the benefit of all beings'. Some groups integrate this with more overtly mythological concerns, such as the Sun Dancers of San Rafael, California, who describe themselves in their advertising as a dance company which 'celebrates the magical force and wonder of the female and dedicates its artistic and teaching endeavors to the dignity and empowerment of all life and to the preservation of Mother Earth'.

Others who seek for personal transformation may look to more evidently 'religious' practices such as channelling and past-life therapies as a means of expanding their consciousness. These are the techniques that tend to grab the headlines whenever New Age is being discussed. But some now claim that such experiences can be produced by purely technological methods, and in recent years the market has been flooded by a bewildering array of so-called electronic mind machines. The inventors of these devices claim that by a mixture of visual and aural stimuli they can induce subtle changes in brain wave patterns, leading to altered states of consciousness that can enhance creativity, influence moods, impart greater powers of concentration, speed up learning processes, make those who use them stronger and fitter, help them fight addictions and give them a supercharged sex life – to mention just a few of their claimed benefits. At one time it was necessary to go to a 'Mind Gymnasium' to partake of such therapy (a fashionable form of relaxation developed for the benefit of stressed-out Japanese executives in the 1970s). Today one can tune into a device like a portable CD player that, it is claimed, will induce altered states as people walk along the street.

Dimensions of Consciousness

Consciousness is one of the buzz words in certain sections of the New Age. But what exactly is it, and what do people mean when they talk of moving from one dimension of consciousness to another? To put it simply, there are two kinds of people: ordinary mortals, and transformed or enlightened ones. To be ordinary is to have a mind that is not aware of itself. To be transformed is to be aware of the mind, conscious of one's own consciousness. By moving into the 'fourth dimension' of consciousness, a person is empowered to see the other three dimensions in a new way, and every other dimension beyond that brings a further enhancement in self-knowledge. In the words of Marilyn Ferguson, 'The fourth dimension is not another place; it is *this* place, and it is immanent in us, a process.'[13] It is commonly claimed that we do not automatically enjoy this enhanced consciousness because the two hemispheres of our brains have somehow drifted apart. Our lives are dominated and controlled by left-brained functions – things that major on the rational – whereas the possibility of inner knowing and spiritual transformation is locked away in the right brain. To put it simply, the right brain corresponds to the 'heart', while the left brain is the 'mind'.

Within ourselves, therefore, we are a microcosm of the society we have created. Just as there is division and fragmentation all around us, so we are inwardly fragmented and broken. The two aspects of our personality do not know how to communicate with one another, and as a result we live generally disjointed and unsatisfactory lives. In order to evolve a more holistic internal existence, we need to remove the blockages that prevent the rational self from interacting with and being directed by the spiritual self. A transformed consciousness is one in which this integration has been achieved. Therapists sometimes speak of healing 'the wounded child' within. This can be, quite literally, wounded fragments of childhood experience that have a damaging effect on adult personalities. But it can also be understood as the 'Higher Self', an aspect of personality that features a lot in discussions of channelling. In the words of a psychologist who was working with US military personnel:

> *The Inner Child is the spirit within us that underlies all our life experience. ... When the child is feeling free and healthy, we approach life with confidence and enthusiasm. However, if we have experienced trauma, abandonment, or lack of sufficient love and nurturing ... the child is wounded. We become, on some level, dysfunctional ... Together we will develop a system that will enable you to participate fully in healing past emotional wounds, as well as restructuring current attitudes and negative beliefs about Self.*

Since we are complex beings, with body and mind continually interacting with each other, reorganizing one aspect of ourselves can also facilitate and enhance the restructuring and realignment of our whole being. This is where the various techniques for self-realization come into the picture. For when we interfere with any single part of our whole being, that interrupts the old familiar compartmentalized way in which we all live, and opens us up to new dimensions of experience and understanding. Such interference can begin anywhere, which is why energetic sports like skiing or scuba diving can rub shoulders with bodywork exercises like Rolfing or rebirthing as consciousness-enhancing techniques. But once the mechanistic cycle has been broken, things will never be the same again. Self-awareness leads to the discovery of yet other dimensions of consciousness – transpersonal, cosmic, global and universal. The individual self becomes aware of being part of a collective social self – and beyond that, of the transcendent universal Self that is the ground of all things.

There can be no doubt that those who use these techniques as an entry into expanded consciousness, spiritual awareness, personal discovery and transformation are seriously searching for meaning in life. They are looking within themselves because, in a world stripped of its traditional sources of authority and spiritual guidance, there is nowhere else to look. In that sense, much of what is going on can be labelled self-centred. While there obviously are some New Agers who are self-centred in a narcissistic kind of way, that is not a fair criticism when applied more generally. Many more look within to find the truth, because it seems that the answers offered by religious institutions and their leaders can no longer be trusted, and in that context taking personal responsibility for one's own spiritual development appears to be the only responsible option that is left.

Serious Searchers

We need not question the claim that it is possible to enter into altered states of consciousness by such methods. But when these things are treated as ends in themselves, serious New Agers begin to feel distinctly unhappy about it all. One therapist described it to me as 'spiritual tofu: these phenomena are all real, but they're being taken out of context. It's the seduction of thinking they're "it" that is where people go off the path, and to understand them properly they need to be grounded in a deeper tradition.' This superficial approach would be a bit like seeing Jesus only as a wonder-worker, without also taking account of the broader implications of his total teaching.

A significant number of New Age people would disparage what they regard as the simplistic view that is prepared to utilize all kinds of diverse techniques without having regard to their origins and background. The desire to distance themselves from such a pick-and-mix approach is one of the major reasons why more serious searchers are increasingly reluctant to accept that they are part of the New Age at all. There is naturally a good deal of elitism bound up in such an attitude. There is also, however, a qualitative difference between those who think of themselves as serious searchers and the popular side of the New Age. Serious searchers tend to adopt one particular spiritual path. It may be some kind of oriental philosophy, such as Zen or Taoism, or an aspect of ancient paganism. For many, it may also have links with the Christian tradition, for Jesus is widely regarded as a great 'spiritual master', whose teachings originally reflected the radical practical spirituality of the East, which became either hidden or lost with his adoption as a Western hero, and the absorption of his message into the European cultural matrix.

Readers with a sense of Christian history will instinctively think of Gnosticism when they encounter the New Age. Though Ted Peters is over-simplifying things when he characterizes the New Age as 'perennial Gnosticism'[14] there are clear connections. One might instance the fact that one of the leading New Age journals today is simply called *Gnosis*, or draw attention to the fact that Carl

Gustav Jung, whose insights are highly prized in many New Age circles, was himself heavily influenced by the study of ancient Gnosticism.[15] Gnosticism was an ancient heterodox form of Christianity, dating back to the second century AD, which laid great emphasis on precisely those things that many people find absent from the modern church. Not only did it include various mystical rituals and spiritual experiences, but it also reversed traditional gender roles – women could be, and frequently were, Gnostic priests – and it promoted a worldview that, though different from the Hindu outlook, still insisted that there is a divine spark or life-force shared by those who have been chosen, though not by all human beings. To add to its attractions, it had its own secret 'gospels', which claimed to reveal the 'true' picture of Jesus who, in distinction from the Jesus of the Bible, turns out to be a revealer of secrets of precisely the kind that today's spiritual searchers are looking for.

Back in the 1970s, I spent several years researching ancient Gnosticism for a Ph.D. degree in the University of Manchester, England. At that time, I never dreamed it would equip me so well for understanding the modern New Age movement. I certainly could not have imagined that the ancient Gnostic texts found buried in a heap of bird manure at Nag Hammadi in upper Egypt, where they had been abandoned centuries before, would be seized upon so eagerly and would become sacred documents again to space-age spiritual travellers. I remember sharing some details of my research with a New Age psychologist, by way of introducing myself to him. I shall never forget his response: 'Gnosticism? I felt my whole body smile at that word.' It did, too.

He was one of the many thousands who have made themselves familiar with Gnostic texts like *The Gospel of Thomas*, *The Gospel of Philip*, *The Gospel of Truth*, and others found at Nag Hammadi. They were all originally written in Coptic, a hybrid language related to ancient Greek and Egyptian hieroglyphics. The worldview of these texts is very congenial to certain New Agers. The Jesus presented in *Thomas*, for example, makes metaphysical pronouncements that could have come straight out of a modern handbook on self-discovery. Like this typical example: 'It is I who am the light which is above them all. It is I who am the All. From Me did the All come forth, and unto Me did the All extend.'[16]

The texts were originally discovered towards the end of the Second World War, and first began to appear in English translations in the 1950s. The only people who were really interested at the time were scholars of religion, and various crooked antique dealers who made a fortune by circulating the originals on the black market in Europe and the Middle East. The way in which *The Gospel of Thomas* was first published – with the Coptic text printed on one page, and an English translation on the page facing – only served to emphasize its essentially scholarly appeal. It was put out in Holland by E.J. Brill of Leiden, a specialist press whose reputation was established on the high-class production of short-run books for the academic market.[17] But when the same Coptic translation hit the US market under the imprint of an American publisher, sales went through the roof. In due course, when the entire Nag Hammadi Gnostic library first became available in English translation, some 50,000 copies of a hardback edition sold almost overnight.[18] In the intervening years these texts have been reprinted many times, and *The Gospel of Thomas* even has its own site on the world-wide web.[19]

In its original form, Gnosticism was an intensely dualistic, world-denying system. It began from the worldview of the Greek philosopher Plato (428–348 BC), and regarded the human predicament as a metaphysical imprisonment of the spirit within this material world. Salvation was only to be achieved by escape from material existence into the life of the spiritual world, which was far removed from this one and could, by definition, have no intrinsic connection with it. The precise way in which salvation could be obtained varied from one Gnostic system to another (and there were many hundreds of them). But at the heart of it there was always the strong conviction that life in this world, in all its physical manifestations, was a most unsatisfactory way of being. Some sections of the New Age do indeed take the same line, and adopt an explicitly Gnostic worldview, concluding that there can be no hope for humankind apart from a final escape from material existence into the world of spirit. In the writings of Sir George Trevelyan, this even included the Gnostic notion of spiritual emanations and hierarchies.[20] This point of view would generally be shared by those New Agers who specialize in channelling messages from other worlds and contacting spirit guides, or extra-terrestrial civilizations.

Others, however, utilize Gnostic materials while imbuing them with a completely different outlook. As we have seen, Shirley Maclaine adopts an essentially monistic worldview, which one might imagine would be quite incompatible with the dualism of classical Gnosticism. But that does not prevent her claiming that this tradition is also part of her belief system. She certainly shares a common starting point with Gnosticism: human alienation is the result of people being trapped in a form of existence which inhibits the expression of their full nature. But her answer to this predicament is different in almost every respect. For her, salvation does not come through escape from this material world, but very much within it, as people attune themselves to the universal spiritual powers that are all around them, and of which they are already themselves a part. Far from being world-denying in an anti-materialistic sense, her answer is strongly world-affirming, and in this context dualism is not the answer to the human condition, but a part of the problem, as it sets up confrontations between people and the natural world, between men and women, between different races, and so on. On this view, the West's basic problem is its love affair with dualism, and the sooner it is discarded, the better.

This is one of the points at which we come face to face with the discontinuities and contradictions within the New Age, which were noted in the first chapter. It would appear impossible to hold together these opposite polarities. But the key to what is going on is provided by Shirley Maclaine herself, when she asserts that 'Christian Gnostics operated with New Age knowledge and thinking'.[21] Notice that she does not claim New Agers are operating on the basis of Gnostic insights (which would be the historically logical thing to do), but that ancient Gnostics were sharing the benefits of New Age insights. We have already observed the New Age tendency to ransack the Hindu tradition, but in the process to make subtle changes to bring it more in line with a Western viewpoint. The same thing is happening here. The New Age provides the controlling agenda, which arises from its essential character as a product of modernity. In particular, it accepts its own form of the Western doctrines that materialism is a good thing, and that individual freedom and choice are the best ways to exploit material existence. Insofar as it is possible to put that kind of spin on ancient Gnosticism, it will be adopted as an ally in the effort to provide a venerable image for what is in essence a contemporary movement. In the same way, those parts of ancient Gnostic thinking which are less amenable to New Age values are simply discarded. So, for example, while New Age people typically place great store by the claim that the Gnostic gospels contain more authentic information about Jesus than the New Testament does, they simply ignore inconvenient dogmas. *The Gospel of Thomas*, for example, ends with what must be one of the most overtly chauvinistic statements found in any literature:

> *...women are not worthy of Life. Jesus said, 'I myself shall lead her in order to make her male, so that she too may become a living spirit resembling you males. For every woman who will make herself male will enter the Kingdom of Heaven.'* [22]

That is totally at odds with just about all sections of the New Age, yet it never seems to create a problem because it can simply be discarded, even while the rest of the document from which it is taken continues to be highly prized.

Gnosticism is actually enjoying something of a renaissance today among serious spiritual searchers. For a specific example of how this particular spiritual path is being adapted to contemporary circumstances, I went to the Californian town of Palo Alto. Located a little south of San Francisco, at first glance it looks much like any other bedroom suburb, though it is also the centre of Silicon Valley, and home to the prestigious Ivy League Stanford University. The old and the new co-exist here quite happily. While hi-tech boffins expand the frontiers of technology with ever-increasing speed in impressive buildings of glass and steel, others spend their lives delving into the mysteries of the past in the more relaxed atmosphere of Stanford's old Spanish-colonial style campus. But even in the futuristic environment of microprocessors, computers and robotics, there is more than a hint of another ancient and more mystical world. For a good number of the factories where silicon chips are carefully crafted into the raw materials of artificial intelligence are intriguingly constructed in the shape of ancient pyramids a profile which, according to legend, has magical powers to concentrate cosmic and spiritual energy.[23] Here too is one of the largest metaphysical bookstores in northern California – Minerva Books on Alma Street. Palo Alto is also Gnostic territory. The Ecclesia Gnostica Mysteriorum, just a little further along Alma Street, offers to balance the quest for technological advance with an inner search for spiritual self-knowledge.

The publicity handout sounds suitably cryptic and compelling:

we teach the individual to reach the state in which gnosis can be made manifest ... through the understanding of the rich legacy of early myths and symbolism from numerous sources ... and through ritual, celebrating ... archetypical acts of ceremonial communion with the timeless realities of the soul.

After that, it comes as something of an anti-climax to discover that all this takes place in a small neighbourhood shopping centre, where the Gnostic church nestles in a first-floor suite between real estate and lawyers' offices on the one side, and a supermarket on the other. Or maybe this is an appropriate location for a religion whose very existence is clothed in mystery and depends heavily on the belief that there is more to life than meets the eye.

Once inside the Gnostic church, things begin to look rather different. The stairs up to the first floor can hardly be described as anything other than functional. But they lead into a light and airy room with stained-glass windows, and accommodating perhaps 50 or 60 people seated in chairs. At one end, in striking contrast to the rest of the building, stands an elaborate altar. Here the drab functional lines give way to mystical symbols of many kinds, and as the Gnostic Eucharist gets under way there is all the buzz and excitement of an ancient mystery being lovingly recreated to speak again to the human needs of today's world. The altar, slightly raised above the main floor level, is bathed in light, much of it emanating from the many candles placed all around, and is attractively decorated with flowers and peacock feathers. To complete the decor, a simple bronze figurine stands in the centre of the end wall.

The worshippers are a typical cross-section of society, all united by the fact that they find this particular ritual helps them to discover themselves. It reveals to them, in the words of one ancient Gnostic text, 'the knowledge of who we were, and what we have become, where we were or where we were placed, whither we hasten, from what we are redeemed, what birth is, and what rebirth'.[24]

Many such texts are used in the course of the service, but modern hymns and prayers also play a part. In fact, the Gnostic

Eucharist itself turns out to be remarkably similar to a traditional Christian Mass in the Roman Catholic tradition. The presiding (female) bishop wears a simple white gown, with a stole attractively decorated with colourful floral patterns. Other priests, both male and female, also participate in the ritual, wearing surplices vaguely reminiscent of Christian vestments, though with more than a hint of a classical Roman toga about them. Incense, wafers and a large goblet of wine all play their part, and as the ceremony proceeds there is also singing. This consists mostly of harmonic chanting, in a musically hybrid form that sounds like a cross between traditional Gregorian chant and the contemporary music of the French ecumenical Taizé community, together with readings and prayers. Four male priests hold a canopy over the altar, not unlike the *huppa* at a Jewish wedding, while the women priests as well as the wine of the Eucharist are all conspicuously veiled.

'The veils on the women symbolize the same thing as the transformation of the bread and wine. It is a veil in which the divinity, the presence of the extraordinary – Christ, God, whatever you want to call it – hides.' That is how Rosamonde Miller, the bishop of this Gnostic church, explains what is going on. She was born in Languedoc, the home of the thirteenth-century French Gnostic sect known as the Cathars. At the age of 19 she had a remarkable religious experience in a Cuban prison cell, and later joined the French mystical Order of Mary Magdalene. She has been leader of the Palo Alto Gnostics since 1978, and her philosophy is simple: 'Our church has no dogmas and no beliefs. Beliefs hinder the experience of Gnosis.' True to this ideal, there is no need to become a member, nor is it necessary to have undergone any special ceremony such as baptism, in order to belong. It is not even essential to be a Gnostic! Communion is offered to all comers at 10.30 on Sunday mornings. As the publicity handout says: 'No barrier is erected around the altar of the Gnosis.'

Like many groups loosely associated with the New Age, the Gnostic church is not an organization. There is another major centre in Los Angeles, and Bishop Miller knows of about twelve other similar groups around the world, but her congregation has no formal ties with them. They do not all operate in exactly the same way, and only a few of them have evolved liturgical forms of worship. Others are more like study groups, perpetuating their understanding through seminars and workshops that may also include other aspects of the Western esoteric tradition.[25]

Ancient Gnosticism articulated its understanding of the alienation between people and the world in terms of many vivid myths, in which divine personages, angels, demons and spirits feature strongly, in much the same way as they do today within the dualistic New Age which concerns itself with channelling entities, and so on. But modern Gnostics generally discard this mythological framework, preferring to use Gnostic concepts from the past as symbols by which to explain some of life's modern mysteries. The fact that the Gnostic scriptures are not used as a source for either theology or dogma also makes it easier to integrate selected aspects of the world-denying dualistic Gnostic worldview with what would otherwise be an incompatible world-affirming monistic perspective. The resulting synthesis leads to the kind of analysis that is commonplace in New Age spirituality. We are all outsiders in a meaningless world, trapped in systems and societies which create division and disharmony among people and, ultimately, prevent us from relating to the spiritual side of existence, through which alone we can achieve true meaning and satisfaction. Such meaning is to be discovered by ignoring the false images of the world as we know it, and finding the common identity between our own innermost self and the spiritual power of the cosmos.

This has some striking similarities to Jungian psychology, as well as significant connections with the modern Western tradition of existential philosophy. It also provides an easy answer to the age-old problem of pain and suffering. The traditional Christian explanation has been that God made things good, and people have made a mess of the world. But the modern Gnostic simply accepts pain and suffering as an unavoidable tragedy that is an integral part of life itself. It is not God's fault. Nor is it our fault. In fact, the true God is as much an alien in this world as we are. From this vantage point, the world itself is an illusion, and only a rekindled spiritual vision can give it reality and meaning. That is why true knowledge is not a matter of knowing theology, or holding to certain beliefs, but of knowing oneself.

When I met him, Lance Beizer was presiding bishop of the Ecclesia Mystica Sacramentorum in San Jose, California, as well as being a lawyer. He explained his faith as follows:

> When I found the Gnostic church, it was one that resonated well within me as a church which provided me the ritual, the contact with God, the way through the Eucharist service to my soul, without binding me into any kind of demand that I adhere to a particular doctrinal position.

For Bishop Rosamonde Miller,

> Gnosis is a knowledge of the heart. It is not a knowledge that can be imposed. We all have the equipment and the capability for it, but we have been deprived from the ability to recognize the spiritual frame of reference, which is constantly within and around us.

The problem is that we are ignorant of ourselves, and to achieve salvation and wholeness we need to break through this ignorance and into full spiritual consciousness. The ritual of the Gnostic Eucharist is one way to do this. Though the externals of bread and wine are the same as those used in mainline Christian churches, the theology is different. So is the experience, for instead of being a celebration and a commemoration of an event that happened two thousand years ago, the Gnostic Eucharist has a timeless quality about it. As one worshipper commented, 'It's an experience that's happening right now and in this place, and we're living it.'

In addition to the private, internal experiences that the worshippers have as they go within themselves in this way, the actual symbolism of the ceremony also conveys an image of a new age of harmony and peace. Most obviously, perhaps, this is manifested in the way women play a full and equal role with men – not only in the ritual, but in all the images and metaphors used to describe the ultimate spiritual reality of God. The balance of the masculine and feminine principles as a way of getting the cosmos right is an important aspect of Gnostic thinking, just as it has also played a part in alchemy, in Taoism, in Hinduism, in various modern psychological theories and in holistic medicine. Indeed, some of the ancient Gnostic texts have a woman – Mary Magdalene – among the apostles of Christ. For psychoanalyst June Singer, a long-time worshipper with the Palo Alto Gnostics and a Gnostic scholar of some reputation, this is one of its most appealing features:

> *I found something I had been wanting for a long time in a religion – a place where I could feel as a woman an active equal participant not only in the service itself but in the philosophy behind the service.*

If all this is difficult to communicate in words, then that also is part of the package. For the experience of self-discovery is not one that can easily be communicated from one person to another. Indeed, if it could be, then it might not be the real thing. As Lance Beizer put it:

> *As a Gnostic priest, I operate as an intermediary rather than a teacher. You can teach a foreign language, or that Jesus was*

born at a particular time and died at a certain time, and that
his death has a certain kind of meaning. But that sort of infor-
mation is not the same as knowledge of what religion is, what
God is, what our own society is. That is not a thing that can
either be taught, or even communicated. The central idea of
Gnosticism is the gnosis kardias, *or knowledge of the heart.*
That is unrelated to intellectual activity: it has to do with the
individual ability to perceive truth. Down at bottom, we have
to make our own determinations and decisions. A gnosis that
can be taught just isn't the true gnosis.

Rosamonde Miller expressed it more simply: 'In the Gnostic tradition, you don't follow what has been written. You follow what is
found experientially – within yourself.'

The connections between this and the search for spirituality
through psychological self-exploration are obvious, and no doubt
help to explain why, when Carl Jung was asked if he believed in God,
he replied in typical Gnostic fashion: 'I know: I don't need to believe.'

To follow a single specific pathway in the search for personal
enlightenment and self-knowledge is obviously a very demanding
thing. To make progress calls for discipline and hard work, not to
mention an esoteric mind-set that does not come easily to many
Western people. This is why most New Agers still prefer to experi-
ment with a whole variety of techniques for spiritual fulfilment,
rather than sticking with just one possibility. In any case, there are
so many ways to 'go within' that different people are likely to have
their own favourite method. Even one individual, with changing
moods and experiences, may well find that different things appeal
at different stages of life. In this spiritual search, the important
thing is to do what feels right just now. What feels right at some
other time may be completely different.

Whatever the purists within the New Age movement may wish,
it is impossible to deny that at the present time there are relatively

few people who are prepared to stick to a particular spiritual path for too long. In a culture which has encouraged us to expect that anything can be produced almost instantaneously – from coffee to global communications – it is not surprising that instant spirituality should have a strong appeal. Its attractiveness is only heightened when it has every appearance of coming in from some other world than the one we normally inhabit. At one time, extra-terrestrials, spirit guides, near-death experiences, astral projection and past-life recall would all have sounded like something unreal out of a science-fiction thriller. Despite the best efforts of the more reflective leaders of the New Age to persuade us that this is not the centre of things, but is an artificial construct hyped up by self-serving publicity seekers, this is still where much of the interest in New Age is focused. It is also where a lot of money is being made. This is the territory which we move on to explore in our next chapter.

Chapter Four

Searching for the Unknown

From the very beginning of time, people have been fascinated by the possibility that there is more to life than the things we can touch, see, and handle. Could there be some other world out there which, though apparently intangible, yet has an extensive and powerful influence on what goes on in the world as we all know it? Throughout recorded history, the overwhelming majority of the world's people have answered that question with a resounding 'Yes!' Some have developed very specific ideas about what happens in such a world. Medieval European artists often painted lurid pictures of both the pains and pleasures of life in the next world. Others have thought of another world in a more diffuse way, as an ill-defined but vaguely spiritual or metaphysical sphere of existence. From time to time, belief in other worlds has been both questioned and denied. One of the foundational assumptions of modern Western culture, going back to the European Enlightenment, has been that there can be no other world than the one to which our physical senses give us immediate access. That is probably still a dominant opinion among Westerners, but whereas a generation ago those who thought otherwise would have been regarded as cranks or even cases for psychological help, there is now a healthy respect for the opinion that there might be other life forms than our own. This may well be due to the increasing awareness of the mess that we humans have created in this world, and the consequent belief that, if things are to change, then salvation will have to come from outside. Whatever the reason, there has been a significant about-turn in public perceptions. The re-examination of the Roswell incident in several high-profile TV programmes and many books is typical of this trend. In this particular case it is alleged that the bodies of aliens were recovered from a crash-landing in 1947 at Roswell, an otherwise unremarkable spot in New Mexico, and after post-mortem examinations of them what was discovered proved to be so potentially threatening that the whole episode has had to be suppressed by successive US governments. Whatever the truth of that individual example, public interest in the paranormal continues to be reflected in popular TV shows such as *The X-Files*, whose amazing success has surprised even its own producers. Much of the current interest in extra-terrestrials cannot appropriately be regarded as part of the New Age in the narrow sense, but the belief in other worlds, and their ability to influence life in this world, both for good and for ill, has been a significant component of the New Age for a long time. In the New Age, this has focused on the technique of channelling, the seeking and receiving of messages from entities in other worlds, which allegedly possess greater wisdom than ordinary mortals. As a result of this, it is claimed that they can see things in a much wider perspective than we can, and for that reason they have a special role at this point in history, to alert the human race to the real meaning of life.

This is one area that regularly creates problems for those who are now wanting to distance themselves from the 'New Age' label, and it is not difficult to see why serious spiritual searchers should be alienated by the kind of money-making stunts being staged by publicity-seeking channellers. It is possible to sympathize with those who find themselves embarrassed to be associated with all this. Nevertheless, we cannot ignore the fact that channelling is still one of the more popular aspects of New Age spirituality, and any understanding of this movement will need to take account of it.

Tuning in to Spirit Guides

My first experience of all this came in the late 1980s when I joined a crowd of more than two thousand people jammed into a large auditorium in North America to meet with a 35,000-year-old warrior from the lost city of Atlantis, who goes by the name of Ramtha.[1] As the show began, the person who appeared on stage was the exact opposite of the kind of macho barbarian warrior I had been expecting. But it was not long before J.Z. Knight, an unassuming female homemaker from Oregon, was transformed before our very eyes. As her voice took on a lower pitch and her physical appearance was changed, there could be no doubt that we were hearing not her words, but a message that she was channelling from some other world.

As 'the Ram' delivered his message, the audience listened intently to every word. He may well be a very old soul, but when it comes to the fears and concerns of Western people living at the dawn of the new millennium, he certainly seems to know what the issues are. The crisis in the environment, justice and peace, world politics, feminism and personal spirituality – all these, and more, featured prominently in his message. Though his speech was liberally sprinkled with archaic terms that would be more at home in the age of Shakespeare, it all came over with great clarity and considerable persuasion. As the monologue concluded, Ramtha made himself available for further discussion, and many eager hands were raised by those who wanted to ask him further questions. Someone wondered which was the most suitable supermarket in which people of developed consciousness should buy their groceries. Another enquired about the prospects for world peace, and whether a messiah figure would be needed to make all the nations toe the line. An anxious young woman confided that she would like to have a baby, and sought advice about the most auspicious time to conceive. Surprisingly, perhaps, that very personal enquiry received as specific an answer as the question about the supermarket, with precise details not only of the month, but also the day of the month, and even the time of day. In the face of such prodigious knowledge, there is naturally no shortage of questions. As the question time drew to a conclusion, personal consultations were offered to those who wished to pursue matters further. All this came at a price, of course, but that did not seem to deter potential clients.

People whose only spiritual diet has been traditional Western Christianity find all this somewhat far-fetched and unbelievable. But when entities speak, people sit up and take notice. During a 1988 tour of Australia, when Ramtha delivered a warning in the ballroom of the Hyatt-Kingsgate Hotel in Sydney that a tidal wave 'higher than your highest building' would flood over the city, many of the audience went straight out to sell their homes and move to higher ground. Ramtha is just one particularly high-profile example of New Age channelling. Unlikely as it might seem, the fact is that thousands of people all over the world are in daily contact with such spirit guides. Their advice is sought not only at times of crisis but on a regular basis, as a source of empowerment for daily living. There are spirit guides to advise on relationships, goal setting, health, careers advice – and more besides. They can just as easily be consulted over the phone or at sites on the world-wide web as by personal attendance at a large channelling session. Kay Brockway channels an entity called Michael, who she described to me as 'an entity of 1,050 souls who have finished their work in physical bodies and now reside on the Causal Plane'. She went on to explain that the messages she channels bring 'a unique philosophy of understanding our personal essence and personality ... of great assistance in supporting your truth by helping you move through obstructions to higher self-esteem and prosperity'. There is a bewildering variety of such channelled entities, and channellers claim to be receiving cosmic wisdom from dolphins and fairies, as well as beings from past lives and extra-terrestrials from other planets. Some are even beings from the future. They might as easily include the rich and famous as well as the unknown and esoteric. There are channellers who will claim to be able to put their clients in contact with celebrities as varied as John Lennon, John the Apostle, Rembrandt, Abraham Lincoln and Princess Diana. Some entities even dictate books. *A Course on Miracles* is one of the largest and most popular of today's channelled books. First published in 1975 in three volumes, it contains almost 700 pages of basic text, accompanied by a student handbook and a teacher's manual. It was received in a trance by New York psychologist Helen Schucman between 1965 and 1972, and is alleged to contain messages from, among others, no less a figure than Jesus Christ.[2] Other channelled books are less well known, but no less popular – like the material from an entity called Seth, first received back in the sixties and seventies by Jane Roberts but subsequently received by other channellers as well.[3] One that became a best-seller consisted of messages from a bird.[4] The popularity of such works is no doubt related to the deep disillusionment that many people have with merely human opinions on the crises now facing the human race. In his book *Conscious Evolution*, Barry McWaters expresses it like this:

> *We are listening for messages of guidance from every possible source; tuning in our astro-radios, talking to dolphins, and listening more and more attentively to the words of those among us with psychic abilities. Is there help out there? Is there guidance in here? Will anyone respond?*[5]

Shirley Maclaine, though, highlights the status of such extra-terrestrial guides when she reports the advice of a disembodied entity called John:

> *they are operating ... on a higher level of awareness and a higher level of technology also. But they are not to be revered as Godlike. They are merely teachers ... They appear when they are most needed. They serve as a symbol of hope and higher under-standing.*[6]

What are these spiritual entities allegedly saying? Despite the extra-ordinary diversity of such spirit guides, their communications are surprisingly stereotyped. They typically speak in somewhat archaic language (almost invariably English), with a stilted and hesitating form of delivery that demands considerable concentration on the part of their hearers. The messages being delivered also have an amazing similarity, usually assuring humans that this world in which we now exist is not the only one.

In fact, it is not the highest order of reality at all, and existing as we all now do on the 'physical plane' is actually a very limited form of experience. We are all part and parcel of a much larger meta-physical and spiritual world. Insofar as there is a supreme being, 'God' can probably best be described as the source and power behind the entire cosmos. In essence, we are all spiritual beings – only, in contrast to other such beings, we happen to be in bodies just now. We are a part of the absolutely Infinite, which means we have no limitations apart from those we create. That means we choose to be who we now are. The rhetoric is similar to the Human Potential Movement, only taken to more radical conclu-sions. For we will also continue to choose other existences in the future. This present life is only a tiny part of the much larger ongo-ing cycle of spiritual experience in which we are all engaged. The life we live now is not necessarily the only life we ever have lived –

or are ever likely to live. Rebecca Pratt, owner of a crystal store in West Chester County, Pennsylvania, channels an entity called Dameon, and summarized his message for me in a few well-chosen words: 'The entire universe is God. We are part of that God energy. Because of that, we create our own reality.'

Many channelled messages reveal that souls exist at different levels of cosmic wisdom. There are baby souls, young souls, mature souls and old souls – each representing a higher and more advanced level of wisdom than those in previous levels. The individual's soul (or, more properly, the spiritual core of his or her being – sometimes labelled the 'Higher Self') consciously chooses whatever he or she will be and do at any given point in time. From the timeless perspective of the cosmic world of spirit, this means that individuals can (and do) choose to be whoever they wish to be. And they can stick with it for as long or as short a time as they please. Everyone therefore has absolute power over how any given incarnate life works out – choosing not only the moment of their birth, but also that of death, as well as all the events in between. As Henry Ford once said, 'If you think you can, or you think you can't – you're right.'

In this frame of reference, it might appear that being on the physical plane in a body would be a somewhat restrictive experience. But, according to the spirit guides, it need not be. Some people do seem to get locked into what is often called 'negative *karma*', whereby they constantly make unhelpful choices for themselves. But there is no necessity for it to be like that. For each individual soul is an integral part of the great cosmic Soul, which is absolutely infinite. Through this connection, all the wisdom and energy there has ever been is available to guide and direct ordinary humans in the here and now. It is possible to tune in to these sources, often called the Akashic Records, through channelling. Shirley Maclaine's 'John' explains it this way: 'This stored energy called the Akashic Records is as vast scrolls heaped in vast libraries.

You, as an individual, would be thought of as a single scroll within the libraries, or as a single soul within the mind of God.'[7] In one sense, therefore, tuning in to the Akashic Records can also be thought of as tuning in to another dimension of oneself. Typically, people can do this by keeping in constant contact with their own personal 'spirit guides' – entities chosen by the 'Higher Self' before an individual came into this particular life, and to whom they would relate during this experience of incarnate existence. They are a kind of cosmic conscience, available to redirect people towards the fulfilment of their ultimate spiritual goals, and at the same time empowering them to overcome the negative influences that might conspire against that achievement.

Origins

Those with a sense of history, or a knowledge of religious traditions around the world, will recognize that there is nothing particularly new in all this. People allowing themselves to be 'possessed' by allegedly spiritual forces can be found in many religious traditions. Witch-doctors, shamans and fortune-tellers have been around for a very long time, and in cultural contexts as varied as the world itself. Mediums of one sort or another are commonplace even in Western society, quite separately from any influence the New Age might be exerting. However, the New Age manifestation of this has some distinctive elements about it. The word 'channelling' itself, for example, is used to distinguish New Age practices from the work of old-fashioned mediums. Whereas mediums typically communicate with the dead (who generally retain the characteristics of their past human life-forms), New Agers are generally aiming to get in tune with some greater cosmic intelligence that may have no direct connection at all with life as we know it. The entity 'Bashar', for example, channelled by Darryl Anka, is said to be an extra-terrestrial from the planet Essassani. There is, of course, no such planet as this in accepted maps of the solar system – but its existence is said to be assured because of revelations made by Bashar when his spaceship flew over Los Angeles, and which explained that Essassani cannot normally be seen because it exists in a different 'vibrational plane'.

People with a modern Western 'scientific' worldview might be forgiven for treating all this with a good deal of scepticism. At one level, the debate over the possible existence of extra-terrestrials is nothing new, and has been going on more or less throughout history. In ancient Greece, Epicurean and Aristotelian philosophers were talking about it long before the Christian era. It was much discussed in the early centuries of the Christian church, though most Christian writers of the time rejected the possibility that there could be other rational beings out there. By the thirteenth and fourteenth centuries, however, even Christians were reopening the matter, as the writings of previously unexplored ancient civilizations became more accessible. But following the discoveries of people like Galileo and Copernicus, the concept lost much of its attraction, and it came to be taken for granted that no intelligent person could possibly believe in the existence of other worlds.

But interest in it has never completely been extinguished, even among scientists. In his 1871 presidential address to the British Association for the Advancement of Science, Sir William Thomson (Lord Kelvin) spoke in these terms of the origins of life itself:

> *because we all confidently believe that there are at present, and have been from time immemorial, many worlds of life besides our own, we must regard it as probable in the highest degree that there are countless seed-bearing meteoric stones moving about through space ... The hypothesis that life originated on this earth through moss-grown fragments from the ruins of another world may seem wild and visionary; all I maintain is that it is not unscientific.*

Such a claim was greeted with both amazement and amusement by the scientific community of his day. But Thomson continued to hold this view throughout his life. Indeed, he amalgamated it with a Darwinian view of evolution, which only served to give it additional credibility. Thomson himself never seems to have speculated on how we might use our extra-terrestrial connections to improve life today, but no less a figure than Stephen Hawking has lent his support to the idea that such an enterprise would be worthwhile, even if the time travel that he believes would make it possible cannot as yet be engineered:

> *Einstein's general theory of relativity allows the possibility for a way around this difficulty [of time travel]: one might be able to warp spacetime and create a shortcut between the places one wanted to visit ... such warping might be within our capabilities in the future ... to confine our attention to terrestrial matters would be to limit the human spirit.[8]*

It is only a short step from this belief to thinking that, if the human race has gone wrong, then a return to our extra-terrestrial roots for advice will be the way to get things right again. This assumption has inspired many recent movies: *Superman, ET, Altered States, Always, The Day of the Dolphin*, and *The X-Files*, to name but a few.

Not only have scientists found themselves irresistibly drawn to such speculation, but interest in the subject has regularly surfaced in the mainstream religious traditions of Western culture. Recent centuries have seen a whole range of groups loosely affiliated to the Christian tradition, in which encounters with extra-terrestrial guides play a major role. Baron Emanuel Swedenborg was born in Stockholm in 1688, then settled in London in 1747 where he had many unusual experiences, which he described in the preface to his eight-volume *Arcana Coelestia*, written in Latin between 1749 and 1756: 'It has been granted me now for some years to be constantly and uninterruptedly in company with spirits and angels, hearing them speak and in turn speaking with them.' He apparently made correct predictions of some striking earthly events, including a big fire in Stockholm, and his own death – all of it on the basis of information received from his extra-terrestrial guides.

Like J.Z. Knight, the Rev. Thomas Lake Harris (1823–1906) began as a Baptist, but following his encounter with Swedenborgian ideas around 1850, he too committed himself to the quest for contact with extra-terrestrial entities, and subsequently dictated a channelled book-length poem called *An Epic of the Starry Heaven*. He describes his experience in these lines:

> *A new-born language trembled on my tongue,*
> *Whose tones accorded with the singing stars;*
> *A company of spirits, blithe and young*
> *From Jupiter, and Mercury, and Mars,*
> *Drew near and said to me, 'Three days, dear friend,*
> *Thou art our guest; come, wing thy blessed flight*
> *Through the unavailing ocean of sweet light.'*

Ellen G. Harmon (1827–1915) also received such visions. Her husband, James White, was a Baptist minister and a friend of one William Miller, who predicted that Christ would return in either 1843 or 1844. When it failed to happen, this 'Great Disappointment' was explained by reference to the belief in another world. Christ had in fact moved, they claimed – on 22 October 1844 – but only in a cosmic dimension, which was why no one saw him. In reality, though, he had entered the most holy region of the heavens, in order to get ready for his second coming to the earth, which would soon begin. In late 1844, influenced by this belief, Ellen White began to have visions – and in due course she met with extra-terrestrials. She publicized her experiences through a magazine called *The Present Truth*, and in the edition for August 1849 gave the following description of what happened:

> *The Lord has given me a view of other worlds. Wings were given me, and an angel attended me from the city to a place that was bright and glorious. The grass of the place was living green, and the birds there warbled a sweet song. The inhabitants of the place were of all sizes; they were noble, majestic, and lovely ... I asked one of them why they were so much more lovely than those on the earth. The reply was, 'We have lived in strict obedience to the commandments of God, and have not fallen by disobedience, like those on the earth.' ... Then I was taken to a world which had seven moons ... I could not bear the thought of coming back to this dark world again. Then the angel said, 'You must go back, and if you are faithful, you with the 144,000 shall have the privilege of visiting all the worlds.'*

Ellen G. White became the founder of the Seventh-Day Adventist Church. One of her contemporaries, Joseph Smith, founded the Church of Jesus Christ of Latter-Day Saints (Mormons). He too had experiences of another world. Born in 1805 on a farm in Sharon, Vermont, he published *The Book of Mormon* in 1830. He claimed that this book had originally been inscribed on golden plates, which were then hidden near Palmyra, in the state of New York. Their secret location was allegedly revealed to him by Moroni, an angelic being from the New World. *The Book of Mormon* itself is not so very different from mainstream Christian books, and certainly does not promote belief in extra-terrestrial worlds. But later Mormon documents were more influential, notably *The Doctrine and Covenants* (published in 1835, with later additions), and *The Pearl of Great Price* (published in 1851, though collected from earlier magazine articles). Both of these promote belief in extra-terrestrial intelligences. Parley P.

Pratt's 1855 work, *Key to the Science of Theology*, expressed it all succinctly:

> *Gods, angels and men are all of the same species, one race, one great family widely diffused among the planetary systems, as colonies, kingdoms, nations ... The great distinguishing difference between one portion of this race and another, consists in the varied grades of intelligence and purity, and also in the variety of spheres occupied by each, in a series of progressive being.*

Many of the popular hymns used by the Latter-Day Saints also contain the same themes.

Ellen G. White and Joseph Smith emerged as two of the most influential figures in nineteenth-century American culture and, along with Ralph Waldo Emerson (1803–82), have exerted a profound and lasting effect on the religious mindset of their nation. They all believed in the existence of extra-terrestrial entities, and in the possibility of ordinary people making contact with them. Unlike the other two, who were more homespun, Emerson had studied at the prestigious Harvard Divinity School, and then had a distinguished career as minister at the Second Church of Boston (originally Congregationalist, but later to become Unitarian). Influenced by his discovery of the teachings of the *Bhagavad Gita*, he resigned from there and took up a second career as a writer and lecturer. In one of his final sermons (entitled 'Astronomy'), delivered on 27 May 1832 but never published until 1938, he put forward the proposition that Selenites, Jovians and Uranians possess 'far more excellent endowments than ... mankind'.

As a result of the influence of these and similar people, the Great American Dream has always had both a material and a transcendental dimension, defining freedom not only in terms of a comfortable lifestyle for all, but also as a direct personal access to realms of the spiritual.

Similar aspirations surfaced in the work of some well-known British writers of the time, particularly in the poetry of Shelley, Wordsworth, Tennyson and the romantic visionary William Blake. In his poem *Timbuctoo*, written in 1829, Tennyson described how

> *other things talking in unknown tongues,*
> *And notes of busy life in distant worlds*
> *Beat like a far wave on my anxious ear.*

He gave a more personal dimension to these ideas in his *Ode on the Death of the Duke of Wellington*, written in 1852 when he was Poet Laureate:

> *For tho' the Giant Ages heave the hill*
> *And break the shore, and evermore*
> *Make and break, and work their will,*
> *Tho' world on world in myriad myriads roll*
> *Round us, each with different powers,*
> *And other forms of life than ours,*
> *What know we greater than the soul?*

Philip James Bailey (1816–1902) projected a similar cosmology on to Christ himself, who in his poem 'Festus' is depicted as saying:

> *Think not I lived and died for thine alone,*
> *And that no other sphere hath hailed me Christ.*
> *My life is ever suffering for love.*
> *In judging and redeeming worlds is spent*
> *Mine everlasting being.*

The debate has never reached a conclusion. Some from within the broad Christian tradition accepted both the existence and direct guidance of extra-terrestrials. Others argued that it was essentially incompatible with the traditional Christian doctrine of the incarnation. As a result, people like the American Transcendentalists abandoned conventional Christianity altogether, while others, because of their Christian convictions, rejected the possibility of other worlds. Contemporary protagonists in the debate divide on broadly the same grounds. Those who reject Christianity often believe in planetary paradises populated by extra-terrestrials, who will in due time save us all by direct (and usually benevolent) intervention.

Making Connections

Writing in 1985, John White suggested that 'it will not be long, fifty years perhaps, before "channeling" will be considered the norm rather than the exception ... One's "teachers" or "spirit guides" will be as common as one's professors at a university.'[9] His proposed time scale was hopelessly pessimistic, and already what was once a heresy – both scientific and religious – has now become the prevailing truth for many people in this generation. If it is not actually a religion in the narrow sense of the word, then it is certainly some kind of alternative to religion. According to Michael J. Crowe, author of the definitive history of the debate, something like 75 per cent of the most influential astronomers of all time, and about half the leading intellectuals of the eighteenth and nineteenth centuries, have at some time entertained the idea of extra-terrestrial entities.[10] One of the most obvious weaknesses of such a belief has been the fact that it has traditionally been impossible to prove one way or another. But many would argue that New Age insights and experiences are now supplying the evidence. As entities are channelled in from all over the cosmos, the special effects departments in Hollywood provide an increasingly realistic backdrop to this belief, making it more possible than ever before for people to believe that they – or their movie heroes – have actually come into personal contact with beings from out there. The fact that this belief is so deeply engrained in the mainstream of American culture, in particular, goes a long way towards explaining why, even in our cynical age, contact with extra-terrestrial and spirit entities is still so eagerly embraced by so many as the answer to all our problems.

The works of the American Transcendentalists and of poets like Tennyson and Wordsworth are all a part of high culture, and it took a more accessible and popular movement to put their ideas on the agenda of ordinary people. That is exactly what happened in a modest clapboard homestead in Hydesville, New York, which is where hands-on contact with the other world began in modern times. The farm cottage that now stands on the site is not the original, but a replica of the home in which John and Margaret Fox and their two daughters, Margaret and Kate, got in touch with the spirit world on 31 March 1848. After hearing a series of unusual banging noises in the wall of the house, the family decided to challenge whoever was making them to identify themselves. Something replied to their challenge, claiming to be the spirit of someone murdered there long before (and though there was no evidence necessarily to connect the two, a skeleton was indeed unearthed on the site half a century later). This disembodied spirit also appeared to have uncanny knowledge of everyday events in the Foxes' own lives. It knew the number and ages of John and Margaret's children, even those who had lived for only a short time. Within eighteen months, the two daughters had become celebrities, and following their example, contacting the spirits of the dead became something of an obsession, not only throughout much of America, but also in England.

In the closing years of the nineteenth century, people were falling over themselves to get in touch with dead relatives, and there was no shortage of mediums claiming to be able to facilitate their search. One of the most famous was Helena Petrovna Blavatsky. Her early life in Russia was shrouded in mystery, but she claimed to have travelled the world before finally arriving in New York City on 7 July 1873. Once established in the USA, she set up a group called the Brotherhood of Luxor. In 1875, with backing from Henry Steel Olcott, this became known as the Theosophical Society. She was to attract the admiration of many influential people of her day, including the scientist Thomas Edison and the poets Yeats and Tennyson. Though she was involved in many aspects of spiritualism (as it came to be called), Blavatsky's main contribution was the idea that information could be channelled not so much from the spirits of those who were deceased, but from sources of cosmic wisdom. Following the establishment of her Theosophical Society, her aims were set out at great length in a 1,200-page book entitled *Isis Unveiled*. This was a channelled document 'dictated by the Masters of Wisdom via astral light and spirit guides'. Like today's New Age channellers, Blavatsky gave a personal identity to the source of many of her revelations. She claimed they emanated from an Indian by the name of Koot Hoomi Lal Singh, who had progressed through many reincarnations in order to accumulate such a vast store of cosmic wisdom. Though there were many unresolved questions about Blavatsky's claims, her message became very popular, especially among professional and upper-class people – an interesting foreshadowing of the New Age, which also draws much of its support from the same classes.

In the early twentieth century, other influential characters emerged, who also claimed to have the power to channel wisdom from cosmic masters. Among them was Alice Bailey, founder of the Arcane School, who produced twenty-five books between 1919 and 1949, allegedly containing the distilled wisdom of the Tibetan entity Djwhal Khul.[11] Elizabeth Clare Prophet, leader of the Church Universal and Triumphant, still claims to be the mouthpiece and channel for a select group of Ascended Masters. These astral gurus speak only to her, and include Jesus, Mary, Pope John XIII, Sir Thomas More and the eighteenth-century mystic St Germaine. What they say is an interesting mystical mixture appealing mainly to conservative, upwardly mobile young people, in which right-wing politics and patriotism rub shoulders with various Eastern and occult beliefs, all of it presented in New Age jargon and with a sprinkling of selected beliefs taken from a kind of Christian-flavoured Gnosticism.

Edgar Cayce, who died in 1945, was another American mystic who did much to popularize belief in reincarnation. As a therapist, he specialized in psychic diagnosis of medical conditions, and one of his main healing techniques was what is now called past-life recall. But he was also a channeller, for an entity which claimed to give scientific information as well as metaphysical insights. This is a procedure that still goes on today through the Center for Applied Intuition in San Francisco, where channellers try to use their psychic abilities to solve otherwise insoluble scientific problems. At a more popular level, channellers William Rainan and Thomas Jacobson both regularly get in touch with 'Dr Peebles', an entity which claims to be a nineteenth-century Scots medic and makes medical diagnoses as well as metaphysical revelations.

The New Age movement has produced a fair number of well-known and highly esteemed channellers, whose powers are admired and frequently consulted. J.Z. Knight is just one of a vast number of people who manage to make a comfortable living through these activities. Others include Kevin Ryerson, who played a strategic part in Shirley Maclaine's spiritual awakening, and Jach Pursel, who has channelled an entity called Lazaris into the lives of many Hollywood stars. Most of these people first met their spirit guides by accident – and certainly with little, if any, prior preparation. J.Z. Knight, for example, first encountered Ramtha after a weekend spent exploring pyramid power in her kitchen at home. As she placed a pyramid on her head, mindful of the ancient legends that suggested it could be a powerful

concentrator of cosmic and spiritual energy, she had an experience
that changed the course of her life. In her own words,

> *I blinked, and to my utter shock and amazement, there stood a*
> *giant man at the other end of my kitchen ... just standing there,*
> *aglow ... A smile so divine parted his lips to reveal glistening,*
> *immaculate teeth. 'I am Ramtha, the Enlightened One. I have*
> *come to help you over the ditch.'*[12]

He went on to inform her that she and her family were in mortal
danger, and should move house in order to survive. They did –
and not long after, their original home was smashed up by a brutal
gang.

Spiritual Answers

Not surprisingly, many people who receive such revelations are sus-
picious and cynical when these entities make the first moves to
establish contact. But it is also possible to learn how to channel, by
utilizing specific techniques that will engage with spiritual entities.
Sometimes these are connected with the psychological techniques
used for going within in order to discover oneself. Indeed, for most
New Agers the ultimate answer to the quest for personal identity is
likely to include a strong spiritual component of this kind. For the
main discovery to be made about the human personality is that it
consists not just – or even mainly – of flesh and bones, but is a spiritual essence. Knowing oneself includes knowledge of who an individual has been (in past lives) as well as who they are now, and who
they may wish to be in the future. Spirit guides are the ones who
can answer such questions, though these entities may also be identified with the 'Higher Self', the core of personal spiritual being,
also called the superconscious, oversoul, God-Self or Christ-Con-
sciousness. Shirley Maclaine quotes a Swedish friend as saying,

We are all spiritual beings. We just don't acknowledge it. We are spiritual beings of energy who happen to be in the physical body at the present time and Ambres [a channelled entity] is a spiritual being of energy who does not happen to be in the body right now. Of course, he is highly evolved, but then so are we. The difference is that we don't believe it.[13]

The Higher Self is the entity which can help people to identify their own higher purpose. Through it, individuals consciously chose to be here, and to be who they are – which is why contact with it now can keep them focused on their true life purposes. It is no surprise that those who find life aimless and without purpose should be so strongly attracted to therapists who claim to be able to put them in touch with their spirit guides. Not only can this become a way to resolve uncertainties and questions about the present by reference back to what took place in past lives: it also includes a claim to be able to answer the big, ultimate questions, by providing a fresh understanding of personal identity in relation to the whole cosmic scheme of things. There is an appealing and forceful message in all this, especially to people who suffer from a low self-esteem. For it suggests that they are actually very power-ful and important beings, with the potential to do absolutely anything at all.

Everyone at some time has wondered why they are here, and where they came from. The New Age answer is simple: we are all souls in the process of being recycled. This view has its own attrac-tions, and to the uninitiated may sound like a traditional Hindu or Buddhist belief. But it is so firmly grounded on modern Western ideas that its connection with the Indian tradition is highly tenu-ous, to say the least. Hinduism believes that the form in which a soul returns is directly related to its moral performance in previous lives. New Agers, by contrast, claim that souls make personal choices as to who they will be, and what kind of circumstances they will encounter in life. These choices are allegedly made on the basis of their own perceived spiritual needs at any given point. In his book *The Emerging New Age*, sociology professor J.L. Simmons puts it like this:

> *the decision to be reborn is self-determined by each being in consultation with familiar spirits and, often, a small group of more knowledgeable counsellors. The rebirth is planned ... Such plans include the circumstances of birth and a blueprint outline of the life to follow, so that certain experiences might provide the opportunity to learn certain lessons.[14]*

This means that whoever a person is now, and whatever they might be experiencing, it is all happening because they chose that it would. This includes even such negative experiences as economic and social deprivation, personal oppression, marginalization or a gruesome death:

> *We create the realities we experience, consciously or unknowingly. The universe ultimately gives us what we ask for ... Since we construct our own lives, it is false and misleading to blame others for what we are experiencing ... The buck stops with us. And change is in our own hands.[15]*

This is Hinduism deprived of its moral fibre. The Eastern concept of reincarnation has been disembowelled, and combined with Western individualism and basic human selfishness. This kind of combination seems to offer the best of all possible worlds: providing the safety and security of a belief system that promises eternal existence, but without any demand for moral responsibility. When leading New Age guru Bhagwan Shree Rajneesh ('Osho') died in January 1990, his ashes were installed in Pune, India, in a glass-panelled mausoleum that was once his bedroom. The marble container was embossed with an epitaph inscribed in gold, which said it all: 'Osho – never born, never died, visited the planet Earth between December 11 1931 and January 19 1990.' In other words, he had never really been here. This was just as well, for he once claimed to have made love to more women than any other man in the entire history of the world, and following the 1985 collapse of his 'Big Muddy' commune in Oregon, he was deported from the USA and subsequently thrown out of no fewer than twenty-one other countries! It was later claimed that activities at the 'Big Muddy' included crimes that ranged from phone-tapping to the mass poisoning of seven hundred people. But since he had never really been here, it was possible for his followers to claim that he was not responsible!

Channelling

We must now try and form some kind of assessment of all this. Channelling is clearly a major source of this kind of teaching. But can it be trusted to be what it claims to be? Are channellers genuinely spiritual advisers? Or are they, as their opponents claim, dangerous and demonic? This question has been floating round in the back of my mind ever since I first attended a New Age channelling session. Like most other questions about the New Age, there is no one simple answer to it. At the risk of oversimplifying things, I would suggest that modern channelling falls into at least four quite distinct categories.

There can be no doubt that a lot of fraudulent claims are being made, and some channellers are making money under false pretences. People are claiming to have received messages from extra-terrestrial spirit guides, when they know perfectly well that no such thing has happened. This observation need surprise no one, for wherever there is a genuine market for a religious product, hucksters and cheats soon move in to trap the unwary.

There are many examples of the same thing in traditional Christianity, with fraudulent claims about healings. Spiritualism has been plagued by this throughout modern times. Even the Fox sisters who started it all eventually admitted that they had faked some of their early experiences, and one of them (Kate) ultimately turned her back on the whole business. It is always going to be difficult to distinguish fact from fiction in this area. *Caveat emptor!* – Let the buyer beware!

But not all consumers are being exploited, even when the channelling is faked. A lot of people attend channelling sessions simply for entertainment. It is certainly not quite the same experience as an old-fashioned variety show, nor even a modern pop concert. But some channellers are neither more nor less than good actors and actresses, who are providing entertainment for a particular kind of paying audience. They know that, and the audience know it – and everybody gets a reasonable deal. This is especially true of some channellings I have attended in the USA, where there is a much lighter touch to it all than tends to be the case in Europe. Audiences treat it much the same way as they would any kind of magic show. They know that what seems to be happening isn't quite the whole picture. But so long as it is a good show, they are not likely to complain.

The second category gives more cause for concern. For some channellers I have met are almost certainly mentally unbalanced. Believing that you are somebody else can be a symptom of a wide range of psychiatric disturbances, and it has to be more than just coincidence that many channellers have been abused as children or suffered similar traumatic experiences, which would naturally predispose them to psychological and other problems. A well-publicized rape case that came to court in August 1990 in Oshkosh, Wisconsin, hinged on the claims of the defendant that the woman involved was many different people. His lawyers argued that in one personality she had engaged voluntarily in sexual intercourse, and then when she changed personality a different identity felt she had been forced into it against her will. These personalities varied from a woman called 'Jennifer' who was a fun-loving, promiscuous 20-year-old, to a much older woman named 'Franny', and a vulnerable 6-year-old girl called 'Emily'. An expert witness claimed that the woman had as many as 21 different personalities, and identified this condition as a mental illness that typically develops after a traumatic childhood experience. When the District Attorney invited her to change personalities while on the witness stand, she readily complied with the request, and Winnebago County Circuit Judge Robert Hawley, who was presiding over the case, felt it was necessary to require the woman to take an oath each time she changed personalities. Moreover, the lawyers then formally introduced themselves to each of the different personalities, assuming that such knowledge did not automatically transfer between them. That kind of thing is typical of what takes place at many channelling sessions, where a channeller may typically claim to be tuning in to messages from several different personalities, each of whom will have their own tone of voice, and will make their own personal introductions. Certainly, the similarities are too close to be coincidental. Those who denounce channelling unequivocally would do well to bear this in mind, and to realize that a number of totally innocent and unbalanced people are locked in there, sometimes being manipulated by others who merely use them to their own advantage.

These two categories are not the only things involved in channelling, though. In other cases something unusual definitely is happening – though not so much related to contact with beings who are 'out there', as tuning in to material already locked away in the psyche of the channeller. Many channellers begin their sessions with something that looks very much like a form of self-hypnosis, and then deliver their messages while in a state of trance – frequently claiming later that they have no idea what they have said in this condition. It is of course widely recognized that we are conscious of only a tiny percentage of all the material locked away in our brains, and there are many well-known techniques for accessing the rest of it. This process is not necessarily dangerous in itself, and is part of the stock-in-trade of all conventional psychiatrists and psychologists. What is potentially dangerous is the induction of a trance-like state in oneself, and many of the tapes and CDs produced for this purpose can raise genuine concerns for the health and safety of those who use them. In any event, the messages delivered in this form of trance channelling are generally predictable and self-affirming. What comes out is what was already there. Such messages typically reinforce and back up particular lifestyles, and generally reassure their recipients that they are at the centre of things, and are on the right track and have little to fear.

It is impossible to underestimate the creative capacity of the human imagination, and probably the majority of New Age channelling – and the personalities who claim to be speaking through it – emanate from this source. However, this is not the whole story. In his classic book *The Screwtape Letters*, Oxford academic C.S. Lewis made a very perceptive comment about all this. Two devils are planning their strategy:

> *Our policy, for the moment, is to conceal ourselves. Of course this has not always been so. We are really faced with a cruel dilemma. When the humans disbelieve in our existence we lose all the pleasing results of direct terrorism, and we make no magicians. On the other hand, when they believe in us, we cannot make them materialists and sceptics. At least, not yet. I have great hopes that we shall learn in due time how to emotionalize and mythologize their science to such an extent that what is, in effect, a belief in us (though not under that name) will creep in while the human mind remains closed to belief in the Enemy. The 'Life Force', the worship of sex and some aspects*

> *of Psychoanalysis may here prove useful. If once we can produce*
> *our perfect work – the Materialist Magician, the man, not*
> *using, but veritably worshipping, what he vaguely calls 'Forces'*
> *while denying the existence of 'spirits' – then the end of the war*
> *will be in sight.*[16]

Lewis was certainly envisaging a time when the non-threatening and seemingly scientific language of psychology would be used as a cover for occult and demonic activities. We might question whether he was right in his analysis, but channelling certainly blurs the edges between these two aspects of human experience. Alice Bailey, for example, claimed that something like 85 per cent of channelled messages come from within the channeller's own subconscious mind. But that still leaves another 15 per cent that presumably she thought came from some other force or influence outside and beyond the channeller's own personal frame of reference. There can be no doubt that mixed up in all this are techniques and experiences that in other circumstances would be labelled the occult. It is important not to exaggerate this, however. The majority of New Agers are not consciously dabbling with the occult all the time – and if they thought this was where it was leading, they would be the first to call a halt. From my own experience of alleged channellings of spirit guides, I would estimate that not more than about 20 per cent of them are specifically and self-consciously occult experiences. So it is important to keep a sense of proportion here. There is less of the occult in it than many Western Christians are claiming. But equally, New Agers who deny the possibility of such connections are being gullible and naive. The least we can say is that those who are involved in this whole phenomenon are likely to make contact with sinister movements and possibilities that they would not otherwise have encountered. Satanists repeatedly tell me that while the New Age is not the 'real thing', from their point of view, its popularity is lowering the threshold of tolerance for their own movement, and predisposing people to be more open to satanic involvement. It would be foolish and short-sighted to ignore such statements, though that is exactly what often happens in the popular presentation of the New Age found in glossy magazines and TV programmes. By all means let us recognize that the New Age vacuum cleaner – to return to the imagery used in Chapter 1 – contains many things that are harmless, and maybe even fun. But there is also in there a hard core of potentially damaging practices that should not be overlooked. Contact with spirit guides is not always the wholesome and benevolent experience many people make it out to be.

Reincarnation

Belief in reincarnation is fundamental to this entire worldview. If we are not spirits continually being recycled, then the idea that there are spirit guides out there waiting to give us advice makes little sense. That would not necessarily prevent people from believing in it all, of course, for one of the hallmarks of the New Age is the assumption that things do not need to make rational sense in order to be true. Reincarnation itself has been the topic of much heated debate, but despite the remarkable growth of New Age thinking, it is still the case that most Western scientists and religious believers deny the possibility of past lives. Others disagree, and claim to be in possession of evidence to back up their views. Even the sympathetic observer is likely to be forced to admit that much of the so-called evidence is unreliable, and all of it is, at best, circumstantial. But reincarnation is so widely believed in today that it is worthwhile here to say a little more about it. Three claims are typically made.

Intelligent people believe in it

It is often asserted that many great people of the past have believed in reincarnation, even those who have had no contact at all with Eastern mystical traditions. Ancient Greek philosophers and scientists such as Pythagoras, Euclid and Plato, together with modern American heroes like Benjamin Franklin, Thomas Edison, Mark Twain or Abraham Lincoln, not to mention European thinkers such as Leibnitz, Hegel and Goethe, have all been claimed as believers in reincarnation. Much of the so-called evidence for this simply does not stand up to examination. For example, when J.L. Simmons colourfully characterizes Pythagoras as 'actually a wacked-out mystic',[17] he fails to point out that there is absolutely no solid basis of fact in such a description. In any case, the fact that famous people happen to hold a particular belief is scarcely sufficient reason for concluding that it must be true. History is littered with eccentrics who believed all sorts of bizarre things – and their judgements need to be scrutinized as carefully as anyone else's. They could all be wrong, and the fact that they were either famous or successful is totally irrelevant.

Surprising Experiences

Other evidence should be taken more seriously, but in the final analysis is still inconclusive. Near-death experiences – which are merely a particular type of out-of-body experience – play a major role here. A typical example would be a terminally ill patient in hospital under medical care. Some kind of physical crisis might arise – difficult breathing, cardiac arrest, or the like – in which the patient appears to external observers to be completely unconscious. On the contrary, however, the patient herself actually has a heightened sense of consciousness – though not in the body. The patient may find her true self apparently leaving the body, maybe watching from the ceiling what is happening as medics try to

revive it. She is strangely conscious that she belongs to the body –
or vice versa – but is not connected to it. Others talk of this kind of
experience in slightly different terms. They find themselves floating down a dark tunnel, with a bright light at the end of it. As they
emerge from the far end of the tunnel, they are in a beautiful,
near-perfect, light-filled place, which may be populated by others
whom they recognize as friends or relatives. Perhaps there is a river
or a gate through which they are invited to go, but they choose
not to do so, and have a sensation of returning to their physical
body. Whether this is how death actually is, who knows?

It would be foolish to deny that these experiences are real. They
have been reported so frequently, at all historical periods, that we
must take them seriously. When I was a child, probably about 10
or 12 years old, my uncle had a classic experience of this kind while
in surgery. It was a talking point for years, and I remember
quizzing him about it on many occasions. He had no doubt at all
that something both real and profound had happened to him. But
what was it? Many medical scientists describe such experiences as
some kind of hallucination caused by oxygen deprivation at critical
points in the course of illness or crisis – an opinion that may or
may not be correct, but which we need not consider at this point.
For supposing there is some more profound, even spiritual, explanation for these experiences, there is still a substantial evidential
gap between that and the conclusion that they somehow prove the
truth of reincarnation. My uncle was certain that his experience
provided evidence of survival after death, and the existence of a
spiritual realm of being. But reincarnation would be a stage further
on, and the links simply do not exist to go that far. Even to get as
far as we have, one needs to make a lot of assumptions that may
easily turn out to be completely unjustified. It is surely significant
that at the end of her comprehensive and well-researched book,
Carol Zaleski finally concludes with these words:

> *Otherworld visions are products of the same imaginative power*
> *that is active in our ordinary ways of visualizing death; our*
> *tendency to portray ideas in concrete, embodied, and dramatic*
> *forms; the capacity of our inner states to transfigure our percep-*
> *tion of outer landscapes ... and our drive to experience that*
> *universe as a moral and spiritual cosmos in which we belong*
> *and have a purpose. Whatever the study of near-death visions*
> *might reveal about the experience of death, it teaches us just as*
> *much about ourselves as image-making and image-bound*
> *beings.*[18]

Past life recall

Life after death is one thing – but what about life before birth?
From time to time, stories are unearthed of people who not only
claim to have lived before, but who can remember exactly who
they were in a previous life and claim to be able to describe all sorts
of details of that past existence. Their memories of so-called past
lives may vary from merely having a hunch that the individual has
been in a place before, or met someone whom they do not actually
know, to knowing quite specific details of personal relationships,
or even of previous deaths. It has even been claimed that the phenomenon of 'child prodigies' can be explained by the supposition
that particular skills were learned in previous lives. On this argument, Mozart, for example, need not have been particularly gifted:
perhaps he had just been around for a long time, cosmically speaking, and his skills had been learned over an extended number of
lifetimes. So far as I know, there is no evidence that either he or
any other Western child prodigy has ever claimed to remember a
previous existence.

Past-life recall has become a popular technique among New
Age therapists. The theory is straightforward. If an individual has a
problem here and now for which there is no immediately obvious

explanation in their present life experience, the chances are that they could be suffering some kind of hang-up from the traumas of a past existence. A worker who finds difficulty relating to his or her boss may have had a real life-or-death struggle with that person in a previous life. Someone who is afraid of spiders may have been killed by a poisonous insect at another time and place. Going back to those other times and places should therefore help to sort out repressed feelings and put people on the right track for understanding themselves now, and living their present life in a more fulfilled way.

Most of us do not spontaneously have such an awareness. Indeed, past-life therapists generally claim that it is only children up to the age of about three years who are likely to. For the rest, some kind of drug- or hypnosis-induced trance state is necessary before we can access our cosmic memory banks. There can be no doubt that under such conditions many people behave as if they were someone else, apparently adopting different personalities. But such procedures are not without risk, and it is not unknown for this alternative personality to refuse to go away when instructed by the therapist, leaving people in altered states of personality for days or even weeks. In addition, mainline psychiatrists are divided in their opinions of what is actually happening in these instances. Hypnotism itself is a dream-like state, in which the subconscious mind is released from its normal inhibitions, and the therapist assumes a dominant position. When specific suggestions are made to people in this state, they can – and often do – fantasize specifically to please the hypnotist, and all kinds of hidden desires may emerge spontaneously in the form of an imaginary personality. In such a state descriptions of places, people and artefacts can indeed be very vivid, for hypnotized subjects invariably have a very graphic picture of whatever the hypnotist suggests. We do not need to decide whether this kind of explanation is correct. But the fact that there is so much genuine disagreement on the matter should at least alert us to the fact that we are handling a whole collection of phenomena that need to be carefully appraised.

Other understandings of past-life recall range from the fanciful to the merely rationalistic. Some see all this kind of activity as demonic, and believe that under hypnotic conditions people can be possessed by spirits – either evil spirits, or restless spirits that actually belong to personalities who once lived. Others try to explain it by reference to poltergeist activity. Yet others think there is a simple, non-mystical, explanation, and propose that imagined 'past lives' are actually constructed out of materials that they were unconsciously familiar with (movies, books, and so on). These things then become fantasies through which the personality disorders of the present can be worked out. The fact that there is a high incidence of violent and gruesome deaths among those who claim to remember past lives perhaps reinforces the view that the phenomenon is related to the working out of present tensions rather than the recollection of previous existence. In other words, like a lot of channelling, what comes out is what is already there – but hidden deep in the unconscious psyche. This view does not try to deny the therapeutic value of this kind of experience for some people – but it does put a serious question-mark against the idea that past-life recall is evidence for reincarnation.

It is not hard to understand why people long for a second chance in life. Those with a humdrum existence now will certainly get a kick out of believing they were once truly important. Anyone's self-confidence would take a big leap from the knowledge that they had previously been an Egyptian princess, or an American president, or a famous religious leader. But so many people have claimed to be Buddha, Jesus Christ and Mary Queen of Scots that they cannot all be right!

Moral Values

Speculation about past lives may be merely a diversion in discussion of this aspect of New Age spirituality. For this whole way of looking at things poses far more fundamental questions about the meaning of life, and appropriate attitudes in coping with it. We have already characterized this as Hinduism deprived of its moral basis, and for many thinking and sensitive people, this is precisely the problem with it. In classical Hindu thought, reincarnation has an ethical basis: the form in which people may return to more lives will be determined by the way in which they have lived previously. To use Christian imagery, we reap what we sow. This is *karma*, in Hindu terminology. But New Agers are now claiming that we actually choose our own *karma*! Professor Simmons again:

> *This is not some sort of Cosmic Justice, handed down by a God or the Fates. Instead, it is a matter of imagination and vibration levels. What we think and do ... sets into motion what we experience, then and later.*[19]

In simple practical terms, this means that no one need have a sense of moral responsibility for anyone else except themselves. This raises serious moral questions, for the individual is not free to make totally unfettered choices about his or her own lifestyle without creating knock-on effects for others in the wider community. Most of our present world crises – whether social or ecological, human or natural – have been created precisely by that kind of mind-set. To suppose that the disadvantaged, marginalized and exploited people of today's world have chosen to be that way is not only arrogant and selfish, it is the ultimate blasphemy against human nature. As one recent writer cynically – but truly – observes, 'It's a genuine miracle that, given the western history of oppression and domination, the white man's *karma* always puts him on top.'[20]

But this has repercussions that spread even more widely than that. For the notion that we have chosen our own *karma* also means that rich people can sit in the comfort of their luxury cars and drive past a family squatting in a cardboard box, with not the slightest twinge of conscience. The person in the car has chosen to be rich and prosperous. The others – for some totally incomprehensible reason – have chosen to be poor and homeless. The driver might not understand why they have decided to live in that state, but need not doubt that they are there by their own free choice – presumably to fulfil some weird spiritual need that the rest of us can scarcely begin to comprehend. The only thing that is certain is that since that is their choice, no one else need feel obliged to intervene!

It might seem bizarre that people actually think like this, but in some sections of the New Age these ideas are quite deeply entrenched. I remember giving a lecture on the New Age at Edith Cowan University, Perth, Australia, and in the course of my remarks I identified this attitude as one of the major weaknesses of New Age thinking. I was amazed when an academic who was also the leader of a New Age group spoke in the discussion that followed. He assured me that I had fairly described what he believed, but went on to argue that, far from being a weakness in his position, this apparent lack of moral values was actually one of its major strengths. In the course of further debate about this, he went so far as to claim that suffering people everywhere (even the victims of the Nazi Holocaust) were in that situation out of their own personal choice, the motivation for which was in turn related to their cosmic spiritual goals. Many of those who were present could hardly believe what they were hearing. They were horrified by this attitude, as I believe the vast majority of ordinary people would also be. Not all New Age people live this way, but this lack of moral integrity is certainly the logical outcome of this kind of worldview. Writing of the horrific ritual killings perpetrated by American mass murderer Charles Manson and his associates,

Oxford scholar R.C. Zaehner had no hesitation in tracing them back directly to this kind of outlook:

> *Charles Manson was absolutely sane: he had been there, where there is neither good nor evil ... If the ultimate truth ... is that 'All is One' and 'One is All' ... then have we any right to blame Charles Manson? For seen from the point of view of the eternal Now, he did nothing at all.*[21]

These are uncomfortable facts for New Age devotees, which is why they are usually conveniently ignored. But how can we take seriously an outlook claiming to be committed to a holistic world vision, when it is based on a worldview which amounts to little more than an institutionalized selfishness, with no intrinsic underlying moral values?

Social Justice

This brings us on to a final compelling reason for placing a big moral question-mark against much that is in the New Age. The worldview which we have reviewed here is basically animistic, magical – and socially regressive. As New Agers love to point out, it was once the dominant worldview of many different societies. But its gradual displacement by other outlooks has not been an accident: it has come about for very good reasons. For this is the worldview that has consistently produced some of the most oppressive forms of social organization that the world has ever seen. This includes societies in which women have been regularly abused, children have on occasion been sacrificed, and a small number of people claiming superior spiritual knowledge have terrified everybody else. Those voices that are now raised so insistently in the West – especially among self-styled 'deep ecologists' – claiming that there is ancient wisdom locked away in the traditions of obscure cultures would do well to ponder the undeniable fact that there is frequently a black side to what they are advocating. In spite of all the high-sounding theorizing going on in some allegedly enlightened circles today, the fact is that wherever it has been the dominant social force, this kind of worldview has not historically led to a holistic lifestyle, or equality for women, or peaceful co-existence, but quite the reverse. There is a lot of unjustified and naive euphoria and optimism among Westerners encountering all this for the first time.

The entities channelled in New Age seances are all charmingly positive and beneficial. An advert I saw for a channelling course put it like this:

> *Channeling is a powerful and exciting way to discover the higher purpose in your life. Following your higher purpose will bring great gifts of joy, aliveness, and self-love. The ability to connect with a high level guide is a skill that can be learned easily and joyfully. Therefore, the goal of this course is to create a conscious link with your guide so you can channel higher guidance of love and light, thus empowering yourself and others.*

J.L. Simmons says the essential characteristic of such spirits is to be 'playful'. It all sounds so agreeable that anyone would wish to have a go. But this is a deceptively pleasant way of looking at it – for only a fool would forget that there is also what has been called the 'left hand path', in which more malevolent forces are at work. To be fair, we should note that some New Agers are aware of this. Richard Smoley has cautioned,

> *we have no assurance that an entity is wiser, more loving, or more knowledgeable simply because it is from another realm ... Christian literature has a long tradition of the 'discernment of Spirits'. Perhaps it is one that deserves more attention.*[22]

But it is more common to play down this element. Again, J.L. Simmons is representative:

> *There are no actual demons as such, but trafficking with less evolved beings and the low levels of the astral planes engenders little joy or light or love ... To put it mildly, the lower astral levels are not as pleasant as the higher ones.*[23]

The fact that he goes on to describe such beings in colourful language ('more a spiritual skid row than ... the hell of traditional religions') masks the impact that such encounters can have. Other New Agers are far more realistic about the likely outcome of such dealings with 'low-level spirits'. In his book, *Journeys out of the Body*, experienced astral traveller Robert Monroe recalls an occasion when he was repeatedly and viciously attacked by what he identified as evil spirits, two of whom changed into images of his daughters in an effort to unbalance him as he fought against them.[24] The number of adverts for 'spirit entity releasement' that appear in New Age magazines should also sound some warning bells.

This may not be the user-friendly face of the New Age that is promoted in glossy brochures, but its existence cannot be denied. I once visited a sociology professor in Berkeley, California, who was not himself a New Ager but had given testimony in several law suits involving the subject. I have never met a person so paranoid as he was. He found it impossible to believe I was who I claimed to be, and was certain that I had been sent from either the Mafia or some other organized crime ring to beat him up. He was constantly armed and obviously ready to use his weapons – even in a university office. He did not need to tell me that he had encountered the dark side of the New Age. Others have met it when innocently joining New Age seminars and workshops. I remember hearing the story of a young woman of Jewish extraction who attended a residential course in England, and part way through the event was the victim of a brutal physical assault. When she complained to the course organizers, they responded by saying that she had brought her own negative *karma* with her by choosing to have Jewish ancestry. J.L. Simmons appears to support such an understanding of human existence when he writes: 'Different ethnic groups literally create and inhabit different worlds within the larger planetary sphere. We are all performers in the melodramas we have co-created and staged.'[25]

Those who know the teachings of some of the historical predecessors of today's New Age will not be taken aback by some of this. Helena Blavatsky was deeply anti-Semitic, and Lanz von Liebenfels' 'Ariosophy', which stemmed directly from Blavatsky's Theosophy, was a strong influence in the creation of Hitler's Nazi ideology. Alice Bailey too – though she was no friend of the Nazis – described the Jews as 'the world's worst problem' because, as she put it in her book *The Problems of Humanity* (written in 1947, after the Holocaust!), 'separateness' is 'the source of all evil'.[26] This is an opinion that is widely held by today's New Agers. David Spangler is also on record as saying that those who oppose the New Age ideology will ultimately have to be eliminated when the Age of Aquarius arrives.[27] Reflecting on what this could mean, Dr Margaret Brearley – who was Senior Research Fellow at the Centre for Judaism and Jewish-Christian Relations in Birmingham, England, and hardly an extremist – had no hesitation in describing the New Age as 'a potential new Holocaust'.[28]

It would be wrong to imply that all New Agers advocate violence in support of their cause. Many who find themselves generally attracted to the New Age worldview are horrified when they encounter this side of it. In addition, the fact that New Age thinking can on occasion lead to racial discrimination and strong-arm tactics makes it neither better nor worse than the great world religions. Western Christians in particular have little room to throw stones at this point, and should never forget it. They too have frequently lost their way and denied their spiritual heritage, as we shall see in our final chapter. Before we get there, however, we have some other meandering paths to explore. For the history of channelling is closely tied up with the rapidly growing interest in alternative or complementary medicine, and to fill out some other details of the picture this is where we now turn.

Chapter Five

Healing – Ourselves and Our Environment

Some time ago, a couple whom I had known off and on for several years came to see me. They must have been in their mid-fifties, I suppose, and the man had just been diagnosed as a cancer sufferer. It had come to him literally out of the blue and, not surprisingly, they were both distressed about it. Question-marks now hung over all the things they might have been planning for the future, while the past was scrupulously searched for possible clues that could explain why this had happened to them.

As we talked it all through, it soon became obvious that the cancer itself – horrific though it was – was not their most immediate concern at that particular moment. For instead of focusing on the physical symptoms of the disease, almost the whole conversation centred on the doctors whom they had visited in the course of the preceding two or three weeks. It had been a traumatic experience going for all the tests that were involved, and then the wait for the results only served to intensify what was already an emotionally charged situation. When the couple went to the doctor's office to be given his expert prognosis, they were under an

enormous amount of pressure. Being realistic people, they had prepared themselves to come to terms with the outcome, whatever it
might be. But they were completely taken aback by what happened
that day. Ushered into the medical inner sanctum, they met a man
who looked everywhere except in their direction – who was either
incapable of making eye contact with them or else chose not to do
so. He delivered his opinion in a single sentence: 'This is a real mess:
the cancer is already well into your bone structure.' The hapless
patient waited for more, but when no further comment was forth-
coming, he could only respond somewhat limply, 'This is bad news,
then?' But by now the medic had done his job, and was already clear-
ing his desk to move on to the next case. With a brisk assurance that
they could expect to receive his account through the mail, the doctor
brought the interview to an end. So far as he was concerned, that
was the end of the matter. But for the patient and his wife, it was only
just beginning. Dazed and embarrassed, they left the hospital in
tears. At a time when they were acutely vulnerable, a so-called expert
in health care had not only failed to offer them any real care and
counsel, but had adopted such an offhand attitude that they felt personally assaulted – mentally and emotionally, if not physically.

Other cancer sufferers could tell a completely different story.
But it is a simple fact that many people have bad experiences of
health care, and find themselves out of their depth when faced
with the impersonal nature, the expense, the elitism – and, often,
the ineffectiveness – of modern medical science. In a world where
clinical efficiency, pay cheques and patient hours sometimes seem
to be the only things that matter, what has happened to the high
ideals of the Hippocratic oath and medical ethics? Not all medics
are like this, of course. But the fact that any of them are is a powerful indictment of the educational system that has produced
them, and the fact that such people not only keep their jobs but
can be promoted to top positions is itself a sad comment on the
priorities of the health care establishment.

Doctors have never had a good press. As long ago as the fourth century BC, Alexander the Great complained, 'I am dying with the help of too many physicians.' Today more than ever before, people are taking it for granted that if they want to be truly healthy, they will only go to the doctor's office as a last resort. We need not look far to find out why. Like all other aspects of Western thinking, medicine has been profoundly influenced by the all-pervasive Enlightenment values of rationalism, materialism and reductionism. Two beliefs have dominated this worldview. The first is that the only things worth knowing are things that can be analysed in a rational way. Inevitably, anything that cannot be quantified rationally – such as the emotions – has been automatically accorded a lower status than the 'hard facts' of scientific analysis. The second belief is that things can best be understood by taking them apart and reducing them to their constituent components. In medical science, this has led to a dominant position for anatomy and physiology, and as a consequence doctors have often been encouraged to proceed on the unspoken assumption that a patient is little more than a collection of spare parts that still happen to be breathing. Increasing specialization means that more doctors are sharing ever-expanding information about ever-smaller bits of the body. They often find themselves untrained for, and therefore unsympathetic to, any aspects of human illness that transcend the narrow boundaries of their own primary interests. Patients then find that their doctors either misunderstand or play down their pain. They say there is nothing wrong, or that it is 'just their nerves' – and the closer the pain comes to the emotions and feelings, the greater the problem seems to be. Many doctors feel distinctly uncomfortable in handling emotions, whether their own or those of the patient. In my experience, it is highly unusual for a medic acting 'professionally' even to shake hands or make eye contact, let alone engage in any kind of body language that might conceivably communicate a message of care or compassion to the patients. The studied 'laying off of hands' seems to be one of their major therapeutic instruments, and even those who would like to be different find it impossibly threatening to institute change. It is easy to identify some of the causes of this sad state of affairs, and Marilyn Ferguson has put her finger on at least some of the key issues:

> *Warmth, intuition, and imagination are precisely the characteristics likely to be screened out by the emphasis on scholastic standing and test scores. The right brain, in effect, was being denied admission to medical school. There were no quotas for creativity.*[1]

New Paths to Healing

The domination of traditional health care by this mechanistic approach to people and their problems is a major reason for the rapid growth of 'alternative' or 'complementary' medicine. In Britain today, there are now more practitioners of complementary medicine than there are regular general practitioners of scientific medicine. This is probably the one place where most people first encounter a collection of concepts that are loosely related to the New Age. The average person may not appreciate the spiritual connections of much of this, for in today's alternative marketplace a bewildering variety of therapies jostle for position. Some are traditional homespun herbal remedies, though the majority clearly come from another place that is 'different'. Among these one might find acupuncture, crystal healing, colour balancing, channelling, psychic healing of the astral body and a whole collection of other even more arcane practices. None of this is truly new. Fringe medicine has been popular in the West for at least the last hundred years, and until relatively recently it was largely promoted and practised most vigorously within the evangelical Christian community. This has particularly been the case among small sectarian groups such as Seventh-Day Adventists or Plymouth Brethren, who have always tended to have a suspicion of the establishment line, in medicine as in other areas of life. This is why some of the most heated debates about the New Age among Christians have centred on alternative therapies. Practices that have been around for a long time have suddenly had the label 'New Age' attached to them, and treatments that may or may not have worked – but were certainly never believed to be deeply religious in any sense – have been scrutinized from new angles.

Shirley Maclaine is not speaking from a distinctive New Age angle when she says that 'natural, holistic approaches worked better for me than medicines or drugs ... Orthodox Western medicine relied far too heavily on drugs.'[2] Huge numbers of people would agree with her, which is why they are turning to techniques which are claimed to work in a completely different way. Instead of interfering from the outside with the body's natural workings – whether by drugs or surgery – alternative healers work from the inside, releasing the body's own natural healing energies to bring balance and wholeness, and create a sense of spontaneous well-being.

The sceptic might be inclined to think this is all right for people who have never suffered from any major life-threatening illness. But others claim that even things like cancer can be contained – cured, perhaps – by these same methods. Another Hollywood actress, Jill Ireland, described her own experience:

I recalled the moment when I learned I had cancer. At the instant I heard those fateful words, something in me had kicked over. It was as if a switch had been thrown. I felt myself gather all my forces and begin to fight. The energy was there waiting to be tapped. It knew what to fight. The enemy was within my body. The question was how.

> *I also grasped the healing properties of quartz crystals for focusing and energizing my mind and body. A crystal is the only thing in the world that has a perfect molecular order; it is, in fact, perfect order. Sue Colin* [her health adviser] *used them for healing. She would hold a crystal in her hand, drawing the healing energy into her. Sometimes when I was with her, I would meditate using the energy of the crystal [and] held them during my cancer meditation.[3]*

Utilizing such psychic energies to achieve a state of personal wholeness is obviously very different from the mechanistic approach of the scientific establishment. Even when alternative practitioners disclaim any spiritual dimension to their work, their assumptions are so obviously congenial to the New Age outlook that it is not hard to see why the two movements have become so closely interconnected. For spiritually starved Westerners, the search for health has in some cases become a religion. One of the most widely researched histories of the subject explains why:

> *metaphysical healing systems are almost perfectly suited to the secular character of our age in that they provide experiential access to the sacred while neatly side-stepping modern disquietude concerning traditional religious authority. In this way they initiate individuals otherwise quite at home in the modern world into a distinctively religious vision of the forces upon which health and happiness depend* ... So prominent are the religious overtones of the healing movements that it is tempting to think that they function only secondarily as purveyors of therapeutic techniques.[4]

Alternative Medicine and Esoteric Spirituality

In recent centuries, spiritual and religious 'awakenings' have regularly given birth to new concepts of health and medicine. The therapies that are enjoying renewed popularity today all have their origins with people and events we have met before in our discussion of the esoteric aspects of the New Age outlook. Swedenborg's New Jerusalem Church, Ellen G. White's Seventh-Day Adventists and Mary Baker Eddy's Christian Science all feature prominently in the development of modern holistic health care. It is therefore no surprise to find that religious and metaphysical considerations play a key role in the practice of alternative medicine. Insofar as alternative medicine requires a religious worldview, it undoubtedly finds the outlook of the New Age a good deal more congenial than the theology of traditional mainstream Christianity.

The precursors of New Age therapies can be traced back to the experiments of Franz Anton Mesmer (1734–1815), a native of Vienna who came up with the idea of what he called 'animal magnetism'. He coined this as a convenient way of referring to the union of body, mind and spirit which he believed was a medium through which forces of all kinds pass as they move from one object to another. He suggested that light, heat, electricity and magnetism all operated through this same energy network, and a proper supply of 'animal magnetism' was therefore essential for good health. Any kind of illness indicated that these forces had somehow become unbalanced, and so the restoration of balance must be the key to good health. To achieve this balance of forces, Mesmer used various hypnotic techniques to produce altered states of consciousness in his patients – a practice which introduced the word 'mesmerize' into the English language. With the patient in this state, the therapist could concentrate the flow of 'animal magnetism' to diseased organs, by passing his or her hands over the body, or using physical massage and manipulation.

This general idea that health is related to the balance of life-giving forces and energies, and that illness means things are out of balance, is central to the majority of today's alternative therapies. Some therapists are concerned only with the balance of purely physical powers, such as the influence of magnetic force fields, but the concept is unquestionably rooted in more spiritual and mystical ideas from both East and West. The idea that everything and everybody is part of one universal cosmic energy system has provided a basis for the healing work of shamans and native healers in many different cultures, while the balancing of impersonal energy forces – *Chi* to the Chinese, *Ki* to the Japanese, *prana* to the Hindus – is the starting point for all oriental mystical healing. In this view of things, pain is merely the accumulation of energy in the wrong place, and balancing the energy and shifting it round into the right places will restore health and harmony to the body. As long ago as 1847, it was observed that mesmerized people

speak as if, to their consciousness, they had undergone an inward translation by which they had passed out of a material into a spiritual body ... The state into which a subject is brought by the mesmerizing process is a state in which the spirit predominates for the time being over the body.[5]

Other incidents from the same period enable us to trace explicit connections between such alternative therapies and leading characters in the development of spiritualism, one of the streams that has flowed into the New Age. In 1843, the mesmerist practitioner J. Stanley Grimes arrived in Poughkeepsie, the home town of an apprentice cobbler by the name of Andrew Jackson Davis. Grimes selected Davis at random at a public demonstration of his healing techniques, whereupon the cobbler soon found himself channelling messages from spirit guides, including the dead Emanuel Swedenborg, who, it was claimed, was even wiser in the spirit than he had been in the flesh. He eventually wrote a book called *The Harmonial Philosophy*, which was a volume of health advice, much of it channelled from spirit guides, and all of it based on a spiritualist worldview. In a direct foreshadowing of today's New Age therapies, he clearly identified opening oneself up to greater spiritual powers as the key to good health.

The early history of osteopathy provides other examples of similar concepts. It was founded by Andrew Taylor Still (1828–1917), the son of a Methodist minister, who started his healing career as a magnetic mesmerist. He agreed that health was the harmonious and undisturbed flow of energy, but he also believed that blockages to this flow could be removed by manual manipulation of the body. He advised patients:

> *Think of yourself as an electric battery. Electricity seems to have the power to explode or distribute oxygen, from which we receive the vitalizing benefits. When it plays freely all through your system, you feel well. Shut it off in one place and congestion may result; in this case a medical doctor, by dosing you with drugs, would increase this congestion until it resulted in decay ... Not so with an Osteopath. He removes the obstruction, lets the life-giving current have full play, and the man is restored to health.*[6]

This might seem merely a curiosity of the pre-scientific mentality, except that Still also advised his patients to 'Remember that all power is powerless except the unerring Deity of your being, to whose unchangeable laws you must conform if you hope to win the battle of your life.'[7]

Emanuel Swedenborg's religious ideas provided a coherent frame of reference for the developing interests of alternative practitioners. Relatively few of them actually followed his teachings in detail. But his basic concepts provided a structure within which a spiritual dimension to life could be located. In particular, his view was that the universe consisted of many interconnecting dimensions – physical, mental, spiritual, angelic, and so on. It was soon being argued that when harmony was established between these realms, balance and wisdom could flow from the higher into the lower. Therefore, as the barriers separating people from their cosmic context were broken down, so wholeness and vitality would automatically be induced. Therapies like this enjoyed great popularity among the Transcendentalists. People like Henry David Thoreau and Ralph Waldo Emerson were not only advocates of Eastern mysticism: they were also ardent devotees of complementary medicine. The view expressed by nineteenth-century healer Ralph Waldo Trine could have come straight from a modern New Age manual:

> *In just the degree that we come into a conscious realization of our oneness with the Infinite Life, and open ourselves to the Divine inflow, do we actualize in ourselves the qualities and powers of the Infinite Life, do we make ourselves channels through which the Infinite Intelligence and Power can work. In just the degree in which you realize your oneness with the Infinite Spirit, you will exchange dis-ease for ease, inharmony for harmony, suffering and pain for abounding health and strength.*[8]

Other pioneers in the field included John H. Kellogg, who was originally a member of the Seventh-Day Adventist church, but soon abandoned orthodox Christian theology for the more esoteric beliefs that he recognized to be the only logical underpinning for the alternative health scene. Writing in 1903, he too expressed views that would readily be accepted within the New Age: 'God is *in* nature ... God actually entered into the product of his creative skill, so that it might not only outwardly reflect the divine conception, but that it might think divinely, and act divinely.'[9]

For expressing this opinion he was thrown out of the Seventh-Day Adventists. But he was not the only one to express such sentiments. Phineas Parkhurst Quimby (1802–66) was another popular practitioner who proceeded along the same lines, arguing that

> *all sickness is in the mind or belief ... Disease is the effect of a*
> *wrong direction given to the mind ... disease is something made*
> *by belief or forced upon us by our parents or public opinion ... if*
> *you can face the error and argue it down you can cure the sick.*[10]

This belief in turn led to the development of Christian Science, which turned out to be one of North America's largest new religious movements. Its founder, Mary Baker Eddy, was apparently one of Quimby's patients.

Homeopathy and chiropractic may seem less 'alternative' than some other therapies – and certainly, both have been more widely accepted by the medical establishment. But they also emerged from the same mystical worldview, in which matter and spirit were perceived as part and parcel of one entity. Samuel Christian Hahnemann (1755–1843), founder of homeopathy, described the workings of his theories as 'spirit-like'.[11] According to his biographer, his philosophical base came from the mysticism of Confucius, whom he described as 'the benefactor of humanity, who has shown us the straight path to wisdom and to God', and of whom he wrote in a letter shortly before he died, 'Soon I will embrace him in the kingdom of blissful spirits.'[12]

The father-and-son team of D.D. and B.J. Palmer, who developed chiropractic, similarly had no hesitation in proclaiming the metaphysical basis of their theories. Writing in 1910, the father put across what would today be regarded as a 'New Age' message when he claimed that

Growth, unfoldment is seen everywhere. Each individualized portion of matter is but an epitome of the universe, each growing and developing toward a higher sphere of action ... The Universal Intelligence collectively or individualized, desires to express itself in the best manner possible ... Man's aspirations should be to advance to a superior level, to make himself better, physically, mentally, and spiritually.[13]

The son, B.J. Palmer, wrote a number of popular works (including one on reincarnation), all making a direct link between spiritual progress and chiropractic: 'Everything that man could ask or pray for he has within ... The Chiropractor removes the obstruction, adjusts the cause, and there are going to be effects.'[14]

The same themes are commonplace in today's holistic health movement. The entry on 'Chiropractic' in *The Holistic Health Handbook* has this to say:

the universe is perfectly organized and ... as extensions of that universal intelligence, we also have an unlimited potential for life and health ... In order to express more of your potential, you need only keep the channels of that expression open.[15]

Though still in the field, chiropractic has been overtaken in popularity by other bodywork therapies such as Reiki and Rolfing. Health is regularly understood in terms of self-discovery, especially the awareness that we are all part of some spiritual entity that is far larger than ourselves. *The Holistic Health Handbook* again affirms that 'we are all affected by the universal Life Energy'.[16] Tuning into this energy is what alternative medicine is all about, whether the energy is manifested through physical force fields, channelling of spirit guides, the magical powers of crystals, or the concepts of mysticism in its many various guises.

Therapies

It would be impossible to deal comprehensively here with the whole range of complementary medical care. There are hundreds of theories and techniques already in vogue – and new ones are being promoted all the time. But it will be helpful to single out one or two specific examples, to show how closely the general assumptions of holistic health relate to the New Age worldview.

If there is such a thing as a typical New Age healing technique, then colour therapy has got to be it. In every New Age fair there will be holistic aura-readers, claiming to be able to see clairvoyantly the etheric electromagnetic colour fields that are supposed to surround every living thing. Depending on what they discover, they may prescribe various treatments in order to keep one's personal light spectrum in balance. The thinking behind this is related to Alice Bailey's view (channelled from Tibetan Masters), that we all exist in four forms: the physical body, the etheric body, the astral body and the mental body. So far as healing is concerned, the etheric body is the key. This is comprised of pure energy, and as such never loses its health and vitality. In the words of Djwhal Khul, channelled through Bailey, its main purpose is to 'vitalize and energize the physical body and thus integrate it into the energy body of the Earth and of the solar system'.[17] If the energy of this etheric body is enabled to flow directly into the physical body, everything will come together.

Popular promotions of colour therapy frequently imply that it is only a visual concept that will help clients to choose the best clothes to match their hair or skin type, or indeed the seasons of the year. But the underlying philosophy is heavily spiritual and metaphysical, not merely cosmetic, and stems directly from the belief that light is the major type of energy in the universe. It is generally claimed that everything is light. Even apparently dense objects, such as brick walls or tables and chairs, are really made of light – but light that is pulsating at such low frequency levels that we normally perceive them as being solid. On this understanding, we are all walking energy fields. But light is not a simple energy. When light shines through a prism it produces the seven colours of the rainbow – colours, it is claimed, that are vitally important for human health and well-being. This is why the aura is supposed to cover the whole spectrum of light frequencies. For the seven basic colours correspond to the seven *chakras* or spiritual power centres of the body, identified in many mystical systems (though some healers now claim to be able to identify twelve of them). These *chakras* are located along the spinal column, and each has a different colour associated with it. The correct flow of light through the *chakras* will ensure continuing vitality and power, and will stimulate healing.

The proportions of each colour in a person's aura determine whether the individual is well or ill. If colours like grey or navy blue – or especially black – predominate, then that is bad news. The presence of bright colours like gold, blue, green or white shows that all is well. Wearing the colours that are not strongly represented can help to strengthen the aura. But the same effect can allegedly be achieved simply by visualizing the appropriate colours. Each one has power to induce higher vibrations in the consciousness, thereby healing various parts of the body. So white will produce a high state of spiritual attunement; silver will trigger off artistic and creative vibrations; yellow will enhance intelligence and inventiveness; orange brings joy and vitality; indigo helps control bleeding; lavender promotes sentimentality and nostalgia – and so on, through the whole spectrum. Once a condition has been diagnosed, it can be put right by tuning in to the appropriate colour.

This is all based on the familiar view found in the monistic sections of the New Age, that regards the whole cosmos as consisting of one divine essence or energy force common to people, the natural world and the world of spirit. Each plane of reality expresses the same energy, though at different vibrations. As one author puts it, 'The standard definition of God, "God is light", is just a simple way of saying that God is energy. Electromagnetic energy. He is not a He but an It; a field of energy that permeates the entire universe.'[18]

The same outlook inspires the use of crystals for healing, though their place in alternative medicine goes back further than colour therapy. In modern times, they were popularized by Baron Charles von Reichanbach, a nineteenth-century disciple of Mesmer. Instead of using just the hands to control the flow of 'animal magnetism', he passed crystals over the bodies of his patients, especially quartz crystals, which he believed were particularly effective in freeing up the flow of force fields. Modern therapists utilize crystals to attune the *chakras* properly, identifying different crystals with different *chakras*. So, for example, amethyst at the forehead is supposed to improve clairvoyance, while lapis lazuli at the throat will improve communication skills. There is a whole hierarchy of crystals, each with its own particular purpose. Crystals are mostly used in their natural form as stones. But it is also possible to buy crystal bowls which, it is claimed, will create vibrations that induce altered states of consciousness. It is even possible to go to a holistic New Age dentist and have fillings made out of crystals! Crystals may be used for the healing of specific conditions, but as with colours the major focus of interest lies in their spiritual powers. It is regularly claimed that crystal can somehow tap into the energies of the universe.

The reasoning used to explain this highlights the intriguing relationship that exists between New Age thinking and the modern scientific community. Crystals – silicon – are at the heart of the modern computer industry, which is based on the fact that crystals are remarkably good conductors of electrical energy. But if they are good conductors of electrical energy, presumably they are good conductors of other kinds of energy too – like psychic energy, spiritual energy, even the essential energy fields of the whole cosmos. In a chemical sense, of course, crystals can be thought of as the essence of the cosmos: the distillation in its purest form of the elements that go to make up the natural world. To be in contact with crystals is therefore to connect with some primal life forces of the earth, and because of this crystals can provide an ideal way of aligning personal energy with cosmic energy. In the words of Korra Deaver:

> *Crystals act as transformers and harmonizers of energy. Illness in the physical body is a reflection of disruption or disharmony of energies in the etheric body, and healing takes place when harmony is restored to the subtler bodies. The crystal acts as a focus of healing energy and healing intent, and thereby produces the appropriate energy.*[19]

Because this cosmic energy is perfect and all-embracing, any kind of weakness or negative influences in the human body can be strengthened and corrected by tapping into it through crystals.

Of course, it is not essential to use anything other than one's own body to tune into these mystical forces. As with channelling, one of the great attractions of alternative medicine has always been that anyone can learn how to do it. Samuel Thomson, a nineteenth-century American healer, adopted the slogan, 'To make every man his physician'.[20] One of today's most popular do-it-yourself methods – widely adopted even by conventional medicine – is the technique of Therapeutic Touch. This idea originated with Dolores Kreiger, who uses the Hindu concept of *prana* to give identity to the store of cosmic metaphysical energy. In her best-selling book *The Therapeutic Touch*, she describes how would-be healers should first contact this energy by purifying their own *chakras*. After this they will be able to communicate it to others by various procedures in which 'The act of healing ... would entail the channeling of this energy flow by the healer for the well-being of the sick individual.'[21]

This is not unlike Reiki, one of the favourite New Age body-work therapies. Reiki practitioner Glenda Rye described it to me in the following terms:

> *Reiki is the art and science of consistently being able to tap into the universal life force energy to promote spiritual, mental, and physical healing ... The energy flows through the healer corresponding to the needs of the client. The healer also receives energy as it flows through them ... There is no need to remove clothes. Reiki will go through clothes, blankets, and even casts. The desire to learn and the attunements are all you need. Spiritual growth and physical healing will be nurtured by the universe.*

Though she went on to claim that 'Reiki is not a religion, dogma, or cult', it – like Therapeutic Touch and all similar procedures – clearly assumes a distinctive religious viewpoint, namely that the same divine essence runs through people, plants and animals, and the cosmic world of spirit. R.C. Fuller has no hesitation in concluding that when conventional medicine uses these methods, it is

> *not simply introducing nurses to new techniques that will supplement the impersonal and overly materialistic therapies associated with medical science ... [but] promulgating a new world view in which the physical is understood to be enveloped by a metaphysical agent undetected by the senses.*[22]

Health and Wholeness

Health has always gone hand in hand with larger issues in life, such as happiness and personal fulfilment. In his famous hierarchy of needs, Abraham Maslow identified basic good health as one of the foundations for any kind of satisfactory existence.[23] Without health, nothing else is possible, because being unhealthy inevitably places severe restrictions on life's possibilities. But what exactly is health? Is it a smoothly functioning body? Or is it something more – wholeness of personality?

In its official definition of 'health', the World Health Organization opts for the second of these: 'Health is physical, psychological and social well-being, not merely the absence of disease.' But historically, Western medical science has chosen the first. On this understanding, people are basically bodies, made like machines out of many different parts, and disease occurs when the components break down. Therefore, repairing them – by drugs or surgery – will restore a person to health. Regular medical practice normally proceeds on the basis of what the nineteenth-century physician Benjamin Rush called 'direct and drastic interferences' with the biological systems of the patient. In his day, this meant procedures like bloodletting, or dosing with poisons such as mercury, arsenic, opium and strychnine – or even, on occasion, branding with red-hot irons – in the attempt to clear out the patient's system. Such practices were mostly ineffective, and quite frequently fatal, and modern medicine has rightly moved on from all that. But 'direct and drastic interferences' are still the basic methodology. Electronic gadgets are being used more and more to keep people artificially 'alive' when all possible hope of restoration has long since disappeared. This can sometimes go on for years at a time, at enormous cost to relatives who find themselves not only paying the doctors but becoming involved in complex litigation to try and have the 'life-support' machines turned off.

It is no surprise that increasing numbers of people find themselves empathizing with the French philosopher Voltaire (1694–1778) who is reputed to have observed that 'Physicians pour drugs of which they know little, to cure diseases of which they know less, into humans of which they know nothing.'

Alternative or complementary medicine takes a different line. Common human experience shows that it is possible to have a perfect body and still be unhappy – or, conversely, to be physically disabled and yet personally fulfilled. Human happiness is much more than just the sum of its parts, and seems to be located somewhere in the interplay between different aspects of the personality. Holistic medicine claims to be treating not merely sickness or disease, but the whole person – body, mind and spirit. This is why self-knowledge is pretty central to all New Age medicine – and why, in the final analysis, it almost always comes down to specifically religious or spiritual considerations. For in this context, self-awareness demands a cosmic consciousness of who we are, where we have come from, why we are here, and who we are becoming – all of which is invariably understood along the lines of the world-view discussed in the previous chapter. One practitioner described his craft to me as 'Energy medicine, not chemical medicine'.

Alternative medicine redefines the conventional Western under-standing of health and healing. To the traditional mainline medic, healing requires that a cure should take place. No cure means fail-ure, and death is the ultimate failure. The cancer specialist with whom we began this chapter assumed that if death looked likely, then nothing else of value could happen, whereas the holistic healer will claim that, even if death is inevitable, healing can still take place. If dying well is now the same thing as being healthy, then clearly the rules of the game have been significantly rewritten. This shift of emphasis explains why Marilyn Ferguson can identify the rise and development of the hospice movement as being part of the New Age 'Aquarian Conspiracy'. For once we start to look at the relationships of mind, body and spirit – treating people in their entirety rather than just as collections of diseased organs – then healing can take place even where a person is facing death. As one AIDS sufferer put it to me, 'Confronting death can make your life better.'

New Age thinking often surfaces most clearly in preparation for death, and it is not uncommon to find the channelling of spirit guides and entering into altered states of consciousness promoted as a means of helping people come to terms with their situation. Death counsellors might be encouraged to use past-life regression therapy as a means of helping their clients understand what death will be like. The reasoning behind this unlikely-sounding idea is simple: if we have all lived before, then we must all have died before. Mind, body, and spirit are connected, not just in this existence, but on the cosmic astral plane as well. The experience of death is therefore nothing new or unusual, and by reliving the deaths of the past we can prepare ourselves the more effectively for the end of this life when it comes.

Explanations and Questions

Most ordinary people have no idea what to make of all this. For the most part, scientific medicine has an inconsistent approach. It is not unusual to find even the apparent successes of alternative therapy dismissed as due to credulity, suggestion or even just coincidence, at the same time as other parts of the health care system is accepting and using some of the techniques of complementary practitioners. Unquestionably, there are many charlatans at work in holistic health care, who are exploiting vulnerable people suffering from life-threatening diseases, and offering in return only bizarre and sometimes painful treatments. It was no surprise to me when the person with whose story I began this chapter received a letter from a kinesiologist offering to relieve him of a large sum of money in the elusive search for a cure for his particular condition. At the same time, some clients clearly derive benefit from alternative therapies. What is going on here?

The laying on of hands is common to very many, if not all of them. That alone makes it very different from conventional practice, and one can readily understand the benefits of that. But the question is, what does this physical contact actually accomplish? In particular, is it – as its practitioners claim – really about feeling energy flows and restoring balance, channelling cosmic forces into or out of the human body? Or is it a form of personal affirmation that can have such powerful results simply because many Westerners are starved of physical contact? There are countless examples showing that a person's ability to survive a crisis increases dramatically with a physically expressed support. Prisoners in concentration camps have been able to endure the most horrific atrocities as a result of love, companionship and tactile affirmation. These things enhance our well-being. Cancer sufferers often complain of what is described as 'skin hunger'. People stop touching them. This is not surprising, given the inhibitions that so many people have about physical contact, even with the healthy. Any touching is obviously likely to have a positive result for the sufferer. It is interesting in this connection to note R.C. Fuller's conclusion that what happens in holistic medicine is similar to what in other times and places would have been rites of religious initiation. These therapies give to individuals for whom religion has consisted of dull habits and lifeless doctrines handed to them by others both experiences and concepts that turn it into a personally meaningful way of life. Is this why the process of receiving such treatment is often more helpful for people than the actual therapeutic outcome? It certainly helps to explain why those involved in this scene can so readily accept ideas that are considerably at variance from either established science or established theology (even their own theology).

There are many features of holistic health that can only be assessed in relation to a careful analysis of their practical performance. But some aspects of this whole way of thinking do give real cause for concern. The New Age insistence that 'you choose to be who you are' surfaces in alternative medicine as the belief that 'you choose your own state of health'. Up to a point, that is true. A person who eats a diet heavy in fatty foods and red meat, smokes a hundred cigarettes a day, drinks a lot of alcohol and never takes any exercise can expect to develop life-threatening problems. But this simple pattern of cause-and-effect is not what is generally in view. For choosing one's own health is frequently traced back to wider cosmic choices made in a spiritual existence before this one. After all, if people choose when to be born, and who to be, they presumably also choose how and when they will die. They may also choose to suffer from certain illnesses, either consciously because they wish to learn whatever spiritual lessons are to be discovered therein, or unconsciously because they have lost touch with their Higher Self or spirit guides. According to J.L. Simmons, 'Deeply woven karmic habit patterns may keep us chronically ill, or on a terminal disease course ... We may have planned to undergo such an experience in this lifetime to learn from it.'[24]

Caroline Myss, whose speciality is intuitive diagnosis, believes that people's attitudes actually create different illnesses. So, for example, 'marked lack of trust is a very significant factor in the creation of a stroke', while 'All forms of arthritis are created in response to feelings of irritation, frustration and anger.'[25] In the same collection of writings, Louise L. Hay identifies everything from AIDS to acne as having a self-determined cause.[26] In conversation, one self-styled cancer therapist drew the obvious conclusion that 'If we are going to believe that we have the power in our own bodies to overcome cancer, then we have to admit that we also had the power to bring on the disease in the first place.' J.L. Simmons would certainly agree with that, when he comments that 'a being will decide to terminate its incarnation in a particular physical life form when the quality of life is no longer suitable for its purposes'.[27] Even Marilyn Ferguson, who is one of the more perceptive and morally sensitive New Age thinkers, asserts without hesitation that 'All illness, whether cancer or schizophrenia or a cold, originates in the bodymind'. Cancer, for example, seems to be prevalent in people who 'tend to keep their feelings to themselves, and most have not had close relationships with their parents. They find it difficult to express anger ... they are conforming and controlled, less autonomous and spontaneous than those whose tests later prove negative'.[28]

If this is the best opinion that can be offered to a dying cancer patient, then this will be poor comfort indeed. Not only are they left to struggle with the disease itself, but they are also having to handle the guilt that they have in some way allowed this to happen in the first place. Just as the New Age worldview gives no hope to those who are economically marginalized and oppressed, it also offers no comfort to those who are suffering. Can any outlook that abandons belief in the existence of undeserved evil ever say anything worthwhile to the vast majority of the world's people? For a world in which there are no victims is not the world as most of us know and experience it. It is not the world as it truly is.

Questions for Christians

As with everything else related to the New Age, it is impossible to generalize here. I have listened to enough alternative practitioners to know that by no means all of them would agree in this crude sense that we choose to be ill. Moreover, some have claimed that their techniques are a rediscovery of procedures that can be traced at least as far back as the stories of Jesus in the New Testament Gospels. B.J. Palmer claimed that Jesus healed people by channelling energy from the cosmic source that he called the Innate.

A similar claim has been made more recently by Ambrose and Olga Worrall, though they go further and also allege that Jesus, like them, was diagnosing and treating illness by means of channelled messages received from spirit guides and extra-terrestrials.[29] Bizarre claims of this sort are matched on the Christian side by equally weird notions that by going to an acupuncturist or a yoga class, or keeping a few crystals in the home, people can become possessed by demons as a result. This is symptomatic of a considerable hostility towards alternative treatments in certain sections of the church. It is argued that the worldview of much, if not all, complementary medicine is New Age, and should therefore be avoided like the plague. Christians should stick to conventional scientific medicine instead.[30]

This is a curious proposition. There is no doubt that, in terms of both historical origins and its own internal logic, alternative medicine is not easily compatible with a Christian worldview – and Christians who regularly use such therapies frequently play this down quite unjustifiably. But those who suggest that going to a conventional doctor and trusting modern medical science is the 'Christian' thing to do, are conveniently ignoring the fact that conventional medicine is also based on a worldview that is fundamentally opposed to the Christian outlook. As in so many other things, Christians have undermined their own integrity with the easy assumption that Christian values are identical with the culture of modernity. The reality is that the scientific materialist basis of conventional medicine is neither more nor less Christian than the monistically inspired worldview of alternative therapists. Indeed, in some respects a rationalist view is, if anything, the more obviously anti-Christian of the two, inasmuch as it consistently denies that there is anything that might be labelled a spiritual dimension to the human personality, and insists that the body is a totally self-contained and independent mechanical system. At least the New Age outlook affirms that people have a spiritual dimension, however muddled and mistaken the New Age concept of that spirit might turn out to be.

There is an urgent need here for a truly Christian view of health care to be articulated in order to provide a framework that will be both authentically Christian and in touch with the realities of the medical world. In the absence of that, though, surely Christians should be pragmatists. The fact is that both systems of health care do seem to work, at least some of the time. No one can deny that many advances in human happiness have come about as a result of conventional medical science. But the same could also be said of complementary medicine. In particular, both the holistic emphasis that we are more than merely bodies, and the corresponding concern for the interplay of mind, body and spirit, are thoroughly Christian values. The importance of personal affirmation and the need for inner healing were emphasized by Jesus himself. Painful memories and guilt will never be healed by drugs. Much of the healing process needs to take place inside – and Jesus, who knew what was in people, recognized this and acted upon it.

Despite the last two hundred years of scientific progress, there are still many things we do not understand about the human body and its workings, and Christians must gladly accept any new knowledge as a part of the God-given miracle of life itself. That is not the same thing as naive acceptance of the latest fads and fashions, whether they be 'scientific' or otherwise. The energy fields of which alternative therapists talk may or may not exist. Their treatments may or may not work. Even if they do work, they may not work for the reasons their promoters think they do. Medical treatment of any sort is not necessarily and directly religious, though I am quite certain that many holistic practitioners either play down or deliberately conceal the religious suppositions on which they operate. Notwithstanding that, however, Australian author John Harris is certainly correct when he argues that medical therapies 'only become manifestations of the New Age when they are seen to be regulated by some form of mystical, spiritual energy, or when they are adhered to because of a belief in reincarnation or pantheism'.[31]

Healing the Earth

J.L. Simmons calls the environmental movement 'a first cousin to the spiritual awakening movement',[32] and with only very slight changes in terminology, much of what has been said about holistic health could also be said of the environment. Indeed, some writers make direct connections between personal health and well-being and the state of the planet. As long ago as 1852, an anonymous editorial in the *Watercure Journal* claimed that 'The natural state of man, as of all plants and animals, is one of uninterrupted health'.[33] Acupuncturist Mark Duke also sees cosmic significance in his own treatments:

> *The acupuncturist ... brings his patients back to health not only for their own sake and happiness, but so that the whole world may function properly. Every needle the acupuncturist twirls between his fingers bears the heavy weight of universal harmony in its slim, pointed end.*[34]

The same sort of idea – that we can actually influence not only who we are but the nature of reality itself – inspired the Harmonic Convergence back in 1987. Just as people are now searching for personal wholeness, bringing together mind, body and spirit, so in world terms many are looking to find the interconnectedness of the physical universe. Far from being the impersonal machine that Western science has conventionally assumed, the earth is alive and has energies of its own, which some claim can be traced and measured. Dowsing, pendulums and other techniques are used to do this, and 'energy maps' are produced, based on the location of such things as 'ley lines', corn circles and ancient standing stones.

These are the same energies that alternative medics often speak of, and some New Agers do not hesitate to give them personal characteristics. I once heard them described as 'the veins and arteries of the earth's nervous system', an image that, if not inspired by, is at least compatible with scientist James E. Lovelock's understanding of the earth as one interlocking symbiotic system, with people as just a part of it. Though he claimed to have no interest in real or imaginary spiritual dimensions of his theory, by introducing the term 'Gaia' as an appropriate label for it, he thereby gave the environmental movement a spiritual dimension. For Gaia was the name of the Earth Mother in ancient Greek mythology.[35]

Some want to understand all this in the most literal form imaginable. If the whole world of nature has a life of its own, perhaps the ancient Greeks got it right after all. Dorothy Maclean, one of the founders of the Findhorn Community, certainly thought so. In a message from spirit guides received in 1963, she was told to

> co-operate in the garden by thinking about the Nature Spirits ... the Spirits of different physical forms, such as the spirits of the clouds, of rain, of the separate vegetables. In the new world their realm will be quite open to humans – or, should I say, humans will be quite open to them.[36]

Just how open was subsequently revealed by Robert Ogilvie Crombie, who in 1966 claimed to have met the Greek god Pan in the garden at Findhorn. After a conversation with this ancient god, he was instructed to preserve a wild area there for the benefit of these nature spirits.

Not all New Agers would go that far. But many are trying to redefine the nature of the earth in some kind of spiritual terms, often by talking of an earth goddess. It has come to be an unquestioned assumption that picturing God as masculine is a root cause of environmental destruction, and that nature is essentially feminine in character. When that is connected to the view that male ways of looking at things allegedly lead to fragmentation and confrontation, in contrast to the female principle which homes in on wholeness and harmony instead, then there is a significant challenge to traditional Western patriarchal religion, Christianity in particular. A New Age leader in the environmental movement put it to me succinctly, if brutally:

> *The Judeo-Christian ethic is that man is the lord of creation, and can do as he wishes. The pagan, archaic-revival point of view is biological, ecological, and stresses co-adaptive relations. We are in a global suicidal crisis – and Christianity has a lot to answer for.*

Many environmental activists take the same position. But the idea that Christians are to blame for the mess the world is in is, at best, naive and uninformed. Quite often, it is deliberately malicious.[37] People of all religions and none have done their share. We have all treated the natural world as just the raw material for technological progress, in the process reducing it to a collection of spare parts for our own consumption. The problem is not related to religious systems: it is deeply ingrained in human nature, and in that sense we are all guilty.

To people with a monistic form of New Age worldview, the most obvious way to reverence the world again is to recognize its innate divinity. For anyone who believes that they, God and everything else in the universe are all one, this makes sense – and if evidence of apparently invisible energy fields can be brought in to support this view, so much the better. Of course, the evidence of energy fields does no such thing. Assuming they exist, and that phenomena such as corn circles and standing stones can reasonably be explained on this basis, the existence of energy fields is neither more nor less than the existence of energy fields. It is a big jump from there to proving that this is some kind of psychic or spiritual energy. Another enormous leap of imagination is required to get from there to the belief that the world itself is a divine entity. The fact that the world is a series of interlocking systems and can best be understood in terms of coherence and interconnectedness is compatible with a whole variety of religious explanations, of which monism is just one. It is equally compatible with the opinion that the Creator made things this way. But none of these religious explanations is actually demanded by the facts.

Many environmental activists are attracted to the idea that people are a part of the natural process, and therefore we will put things right by getting in tune with the cosmos and doing what comes naturally. But those New Agers who adopt a more dualistic perspective have hesitations about this, for it conflicts with other central aspects of the New Age spiritual search as they understand it, especially the concern with self-discovery and inner human development. As a Gnostic, Richard Smoley identifies this incongruity:

> *There is a danger, I believe, in equating God with nature ... man is not fundamentally of nature. The truest, deepest part of him is beyond the cycle of reproduction and survival. To deify nature is to forget this and to put man at the mercy of this cycle rather than to help him transcend it.*[38]

There is also another problem here. New Age environmentalists often speak glibly about living in harmony with nature, being your own truth, living your own truth, and so on, and take it for granted that doing this will automatically promote harmony, peace and stability in the future, and may even reverse some of the damage of the past. But such naive propositions can only seem sensible if we refuse to face the facts of the past. For doing what comes naturally has been the cause of the problem. It is precisely because we have lived for generations by our own private truth values that we have got things into such a mess to start with. It has been the act of choosing for ourselves, without regard either for the welfare of others or for the cosmic consequences, that has led to such widespread devastation of the planet. To imagine that we can get out of the mess we have created by redefining this self-centredness, elevating it to a virtue and calling it 'God' – or 'Goddess' – is naive and unrealistic. The philosophy of doing what comes naturally leads directly to the conclusion that ultimately no one is responsible for their own actions. To observe that we have created our own living hell by making choices that suit our own interests is not narrow-minded dogmatism: it is simply stating an obvious fact. Once again, the weak spot of the whole New Age outlook proves to be its inability to cope with the sheer brutal facts of human life. Whether we like it or not, human evil is a fact, and we cannot make it go away just by denying its existence, or redefining it in some fancy psychological or environmental jargon. Exploitation – whether of the environment or of other people – is real, and the basic issues are not metaphysical or psychological: they are moral. The problem is not the way people are, but the way they choose to behave. Once again, we have to conclude that New Agers are good at asking the right questions, but their answers are less than satisfactory.

Chapter Six

Getting It All Together

The training of top executives by multinational corporations may seem to be an unlikely place to uncover the influence of the New Age. At first glance, the world of big business looks to be light years removed from some of the concerns documented in previous chapters. Esoteric healing techniques, mystical contacts with extra-terrestrial spirit guides and the development of cosmic consciousness appear to have little in common with the aims and objectives of the market-place – except insofar as a few successful entrepreneurs have made themselves rich by purveying the paraphernalia required to follow through such concerns.

But the reality is quite different. The last twenty years have seen management consultants adopt New Age methodologies on a grand scale, and attendance at spiritually oriented training courses has become a regular part of many people's working life. Much attention has been focused on these courses by the popular media, largely because of the adoption of practices that to most people would seem somewhat bizarre. Some of the trendier residential courses might include walking barefoot through glowing coals burning at 1,300°C, or lessons in sky-diving, the martial arts or other physically demanding activities. At others, executives can be found sitting beneath pyramids, or plugged into electronic 'mind machines' which, it is claimed, will expand their brains and put them in tune with cosmic rhythms that will enable them to be more effective people. At one course I came across, managers were studying a book whose author maintains that 'if you simply put this book in your bag or brief case, the eighth dimensional power generated by the book will bring you happiness and good fortune'.[1] In other training sessions, participants might dress up as witches and wizards to create their perfect work environment by casting demons out of their corporate boardrooms. They might even believe themselves to be powerful enough to change the actual nature of reality through techniques such as Neuro-Linguistic Programming. New Age consultants offer to bestow on their clients an almost divine status. One observer of such events wrote of executives coming to think of themselves as being 'like the shamans and magicians of the past ... spiritual warriors', searching for 'a magical elixir to revive the dying dragon child', and thereby establish themselves as 'the initiators and creators of their world'.[2]

It is not difficult to identify a sociological explanation for the emergence of these ideas at this point in time. Throughout the history of Western culture, whenever belief in material revelation (whether sacred or secular) has become problematical, there has always been a tendency to revert to what Aldous Huxley called 'the perennial philosophy',[3] and search instead for an essentialist, idealist (and therefore timeless and universalist) way of understanding the meaning of life. If Western civilization is indeed in terminal decline today, then this is not the first crisis to manifest itself in this form. Carl Raschke (writing on Gnosticism) has argued that this recurring tendency 'represents an ideology peculiar to the latter stages in the demise of the ruling classes'.

In response to a loss of social power and prestige, an anxious and potentially disinherited elite

> *gradually surrenders its leadership functions and devotes its energies to letters and learning ... their painful isolation from the culture of the masses leading to a self-enforced pariah mentality, expressed in both their contempt for legitimate authority and their creation of a closed symbolic universe which only those with the proper credentials can penetrate ... the safekeeping of magical lore reflects a vicarious exercise of power which in reality has slipped away from them.[4]*

Though his particular concern was for what happens when the power base of the aristocracy disappears, a similar erosion of inherited privilege has taken place within the Western business community in recent years, as traditional markets and even, in some cases, traditional industries have disappeared. Alongside this, managers have been forced to become more open with their workers and more directly accountable to their shareholders. In this situation, the adoption of arcane spiritual practices, not accessible to all, is one of the ways in which a new managerial elite can reassert itself. More benevolently, perhaps, the integration of spirituality and management 'offers managers a source of enduring meaning in turbulent times ... and brings profound meaning to their jobs as managers'.[5]

Controversial Courses

At their best, some of these courses can be good fun, especially those that offer nothing more than physical thrills and challenges. But the way in which some of them are conducted has led to serious questions being raised both about the techniques that are employed and about the underlying philosophy and worldview that is being promoted through them. In some cases participants have claimed that their basic human rights have been denied them, and from time to time lawsuits have been brought against the organizers of these courses, in both the USA and Britain.

It is not difficult to understand why some people should feel this way. Here is one example of something that actually happened in a multinational corporation in Scotland, but which is fairly typical of what is going on. A group of top executives had been told they were to go on a management course to improve their skills. Their preliminary instructions were very basic, and all they knew was that they were to present themselves at their workplace early one morning, with a suitcase packed for a course that would last most of the week. They had no idea where they were going, but that hardly seemed important since it was normal business practice for even trivialities to be kept under wraps until the last possible moment. They set off from the company's headquarters in their usual grand style: a fleet of immaculate limousines which would take them the short distance to the nearest airport. There they boarded an unmarked executive jet for a destination still unknown. There was nothing specially unusual about that either, for most company aircraft carry no markings in order to preserve the shroud of commercial secrecy that is believed to be essential for the successful running of a big business. In any case, they took this as a sign that they could expect to enjoy themselves, maybe in an exotic location. During the flight, much food and drink was consumed, and the passage of time was hardly noticed. As one participant told me, they were all enjoying themselves so much that it felt like thirty minutes, though they had actually been travelling for nearer four hours by the time they touched down at a private airstrip.

There were no signs to tell them where they were, and some of them were surprised to find no customs or immigration formalities waiting for them. But they had all been on courses like this before, and knew there was nothing to worry about. In any case, they were obviously not at their final destination, as their jet had come to a stop alongside a fleet of helicopters, which were waiting to take them to journey's end. Two by two, they were assigned to different helicopters, and unceremoniously whisked away. This time, their luggage was left behind – and after a short while the terrain beneath began to look decidedly rugged and inhospitable. They also noticed that the helicopters had not all gone in the same direction, and some began to wonder what had happened to their colleagues. However, such speculation was cut short when the chopper carrying my informants began to make its descent. As they peered out through the mist that now surrounded them, they began to sense that things were not quite what they seemed. They were not, as they had anticipated, at a conference centre. In fact, they were not anywhere recognizable at all. They were just beginning to wonder if they had been kidnapped when the crew of the helicopter bundled them out into the fading light of early evening. They found themselves standing on the soft turf of what turned out to be a very damp moor. They were handed a piece of paper with just two words scribbled on it: the name of the house they were heading for. Without further direction or guidance, they were left on their own. The helicopter took off, and as the thud of its rotor blades gradually faded into the distance, the two colleagues suddenly realized that it was dark, cold, wet and misty, they had no idea where they were – and their business suits were just about the most unsuitable clothing imaginable for their surroundings.

Being people of enterprise (and having no obvious alternative possibility), they began to walk across the undulating countryside. Eventually a road came in sight, and they hailed a distant figure to ask for directions to their destination. That proved to be more complicated than they expected, for the reply came in a language in which neither of them was fluent, and they were not in any case certain that their informant had understood their question in the first place. They pressed on as best they could, and eventually their persistence paid off. Several hours later, exhausted, soaked to the skin and with their business suits torn and ragged, they arrived at the place where the course was to be held. They were ready for a long hot bath, and a good sleep. But the organizers had other ideas. By now it was 6 a.m., and the course leaders had risen bright and early, ready for a prompt start to the day. Of course, they had not spent the previous night tramping through woods and across mountains!

As the first session got under way, the reasoning behind all this was explained by the training team: 'This course is quite unlike any course you have ever been on before. Previous courses you have been on have only treated the symptoms of bad management. This time we are going right back to fundamentals: to you as a manager, and to your own personal worldview and lifestyle.' By way of introducing what that might mean, they were interrogated as to why they had arrived at the conference venue in such a dishevelled state, and why it had taken them so long to make it. Some of them were already a little angry and felt there was a simple answer to those questions – but decided the opening session was not the best time to throw abusive comments at the organizers. When they heard the real answer, however, they began to wonder if they were dreaming. For it was explained that their underlying problem was caused by the fact that they had been brought up and trained to think and live in all the wrong ways. Their methods of operating were too rational and logical, and if they had adopted a more intuitive and spiritually aware approach towards problem-solving they would have found their destination without any difficulty. Instead of being angry, and feeling out of tune with the whole experience, they would have been able to handle their emotions and to relate positively both to themselves and to the others who were there.

As one day followed another, the term 'New Age' was used with ever-increasing frequency to describe the philosophy behind this process of re-education. By the time the course was finished, no one was left in any doubt that what was being demanded of them amounted to nothing short of a total reinvention of themselves and their attitudes, and that they could only do that by adopting a more 'spiritual' approach to life by tuning in to some kind of cosmic power that would energize them for this radical transformation of consciousness.

There is, of course, nothing wrong with testing people's physical and psychological limits in order to help them identify their personal strengths and weaknesses. The kind of orienteering course described here has been commonplace for many years in things like military training, and there is no intrinsic reason why managers should not find the same things useful. But there has often been a subtle difference between military training and the way some business courses have operated. Army recruits expect to be put through that sort of endurance test. But when executives report at their workplace for a management course, kitted out only in a standard business suit, they do not. Many people have no hesitation in applying terms like 'brainwashing' to describe the kind of pressure and humiliation they have had to endure.

Not all courses are exactly the same, but there is an underlying trend. In another widely used programme, workers are forced to endure a whole series of intensive sessions that might last for as long as sixteen hours each, with only limited movement allowed, minimal food and toilet breaks, and no smoking, writing or talking. Instructors regularly humiliate the group by telling them that their lives are in a mess, they are unable to cope and have lost sight of their real life objectives. As the participants sit there for hour after hour, they are gradually worn down, both physically and emotionally, until they are ready for almost anything. People have been known to make all kinds of uncharacteristic emotional confessions – including intimate details of their sexual relationships – and to allow themselves to undergo extensive psychological programming, just to be allowed to get out of the room.[6] It is bad enough to be deliberately disorientated and manipulated in this way. But participants in such courses are then invariably informed that their failure to cope is related to some kind of mental blindness that can only be corrected by a personal spiritual re-alignment, and that by adopting a different worldview and new values they can somehow be reborn and emerge from the process as successful, rich and satisfied.

Religious Beliefs and Management Systems

The thinking behind much of this takes us back to several New Age themes that we have already explored. A widely used academic text that inspires the thinking behind many of these courses adopts an explicitly religious theme. In his book *Creating the Corporate Future*, management professor Russell Ackoff puts forward the proposition that the implicit adoption of Christian values is largely to blame for the mess in which industry often finds itself. Confrontation between workers and managers, the alienation of the workforce, the dehumanizing attitudes which regard people as expendable cogs in a machine – all these and many other negative features are, he claims, simply the natural outworking of the Christian view of God.

This argument is based on a social and historical analysis that no one could reasonably quarrel with. It is pointed out that since the Second World War, the West has been undergoing change of such speed and significance that we today are at a great crossroads in history. One age is coming to an end, and a 'new age' is coming to birth. Until the new age finally arrives, the world is in an intermediate stage, which is an unsettling time of upheaval and change. In this interim period, 'both our methods of understanding the world and our actual understanding of it are undergoing fundamental and profound transformations'. Today's generation therefore stands at a unique point in history, as heirs to the past but masters of the future: 'the problems it confronts are inherited, but those of us who intend to have a hand in shaping the new age are trying to face them in a new way'.

Ackoff refers constantly to the 'new age' (though without capital letters), and much of what he says is unexceptional, and indeed presents a clear analysis of the cultural change that is now taking place. But this talk of a new age dawning is certainly not inconsistent with the populist and more apocalyptic style of New Age vision, with an expectation of some kind of messiah figure who will usher in a new world order – especially when Ackoff uses so much mystical imagery to define the precise form of this coming 'new age':

> *The Systems Age is a movement of many wills in which each has only a small part to play ... It is taking shape before our eyes. It is still too early, however, to foresee all the difficulties that it will generate. Nevertheless, I believe the new age can be trusted to deal with them. Meanwhile there is much work to be done, much scope for greater vision, and much room for enthusiasm and optimism.* [7]

This sounds very much like a more intellectual version of the kind of media hype that has surrounded the Harmonic Convergence and similar events.

In business-speak, the old age we are leaving is described as the 'Machine Age', while the new age that is in process of coming to birth is the 'Systems Age'. The terminology has a long and honourable history. It goes back to Ludwig von Bertalanffy, a German biologist who promoted a science of context called 'perspectivism' which laid the foundations for what subsequently came to be known as General Systems Theory.[8] Put simply, this states that nothing can fully be understood in isolation, but will only make sense within its total context, or 'system'. Each component in any system interacts with all the other components in such a way that it is both impossible and pointless to try and separate them.

Concepts of this sort have shed new light on many areas of modern understanding. The environmental movement, for example, is based on the fact that the natural ecological system of which we are all a part is much bigger and more complex than the various constituent elements that go to make it up. Traditional science in the Cartesian mould tended to assume that the main way to understand anything – from literature to anatomy – was by taking it apart to identify its basic ingredients. Only then – if anything was left – would it be permissible to try and put it all back together again. Inflexible concepts of cause and effect were used to analyse everything, and a virtue was made of keeping things separate – even to the extent of constructing an artificial context for experimentation (the laboratory) where by definition the influence of the natural environment was excluded. It is little wonder that Western culture for the last two centuries has been largely fragmented and has lacked a holistic vision.

The evidence of such fragmentation is plain to see. Many inherited institutions – political, religious, industrial, educational – are bureaucratic and impersonal, operating within rigid mechanistic frameworks that at best lead to fragmentation and conformity, and at worst actually deny some of our most cherished ideals. Following the work of Einstein, modern science began to recognize the inadequacy of this understanding several decades ago, and this growing recognition that things can only be fully understood in their context has marked a major step forward – in the physical sciences, in medicine, and in the workplace.[9] So could it be that the problems of modern industrial structures are related to the acceptance of artificial boundaries between workers and managers, and that the relative inefficiency of both is related to the way their work life has been isolated from their overall lifestyle and values? If taking things apart is the cause of our difficulties, then it follows that putting them together will bring new insights.

There is nothing at all wrong with some of these questions, nor indeed with some of the answers that are being proposed. The difficulties occur when New Age management trainers begin to explain the reason for this fragmentation and disharmony, for they typically do so in overtly religious terms. Moreover, not only does their message offend many of the participants in these courses, but it can also be questioned as an accurate understanding of what has been going on in Western culture. Ackoff claims that the Machine Age was characterized by two basic beliefs: 'that the universe was a machine created by God to do His work, and that He had created man in His image'. This in turn produced the conclusion that 'man ought to be creating machines to do his work', and this belief then produced the philosophy of the Industrial Revolution, which Ackoff describes as

> *a consequence of man's efforts to imitate God by creating machines to do his work. The industrial organizations produced ... were taken to be related to their creators, their owners, much as the universe was to God ... employees were treated as replaceable machines or machine parts even though they were known to be human beings. Their personal objectives, however, were considered irrelevant by employers ... the very simple repetitive tasks they were given to do were designed as though they were to be performed by machines.*[10]

In the process, both workers and managers were dehumanized. Their personal and family life disintegrated in the face of the corporate machine and its many demands – and it was all the fault of Christianity.

If the Machine Age was just Christianity projected into the corporate workplace, what kind of religious beliefs inspire and motivate the Systems Age? Though he gives a nod in the direction of freedom of choice for the individual worker, Ackoff leaves readers in no doubt as to his own personal answer to that question: 'many individuals find comfort in assuming the existence of ... a unifying whole' – and can call it 'God'.

> *This God, however, is very different from the Machine-Age God who was conceptualized as an individual who had created the universe. God-as-the-whole cannot be individualized or personified, and cannot be thought of as the creator. To do so would make no more sense than to speak of man as creator of his organs. In this holistic view of things man is taken as a part of God just as his heart is taken as a part of man.*[11]

The openly anti-Christian orientation of this view is made quite clear in what follows:

> *this holistic concept of God is precisely the one embraced by many Eastern religions which conceptualize God as a system, not as an element ... There is some hope, therefore, that in the creation of systems sciences the cultures of the East and West can be synthesized. The twain may yet meet in the Systems Age.*[12]

These are all key concepts within the monistic New Age, and there is very little difference between this and those views expressed by Shirley Maclaine which we have already examined.

Christian Values and Management Mistakes

Ackoff's opinions are not unusual, and it is surprising how easily – and how often – textbooks on management skills blame the problems of Western industry on what are perceived to be the religious attitudes of both workers and managers. But is it true?

A closer look reveals that this perspective on Western culture is nothing like as convincing as it can be made to seem at first glance. No one would dispute that the mindset which we have inherited from the Industrial Revolution – despite all its achievements – has many built-in weaknesses, not least the dehumanizing of work and workers which Ackoff so eloquently describes. But it is much more difficult to demonstrate that this is the logical outcome of the Christian belief in God as creator. Indeed, it is questionable whether religious beliefs as such have ever exercised much influence at all in the organization of the typical industrial workplace. The drawing of easy connections between religious views of God as a celestial machine-minder and the philosophy of managers is itself a good example of the over-rationalized style of thinking that characterized the so-called Machine Age. Connections like this can seem to make sense in an academic atmosphere isolated from the broader concerns of real life, but they hardly ever happen in the larger context of ordinary daily experience. Most industrialists have been far too busy with other things to spend time in speculation about such esoteric concerns. The idea that the barons of the Industrial Revolution scoured books of theology looking for models of God as a way of improving efficiency and profits is just ludicrous. The majority of them only attended church irregularly, if at all, and very few claimed to be Christian in any committed sense of the word.

Those who did espouse overtly Christian values (like the Cadburys and the Rowntrees in Britain) established 'model' factories which actually reflected many of the more enlightened attitudes now being advocated by systems theorists. If Ackoff's analysis was correct, however, we would expect them to have provided us with examples of the worst excesses of manipulation and exploitation of the workers. From today's perspective, it is easy to criticize the form of caring working community which they created as too paternalistic and over-protective, but the very existence of Christian industrialists with that level of concern for their workers places an enormous question-mark against the simplistic assumption that Christianity is the root cause of the fragmentation and disharmony which now besets Western culture.

Holistic Systems and Christianity

Systems thinking is not at all incompatible with Christianity, and it is hard to understand why management trainers should constantly blame 'Christianity' for the products of modernity. One of the features of much recent thinking within the Christian church has been the considerable emphasis placed on the development of a systems approach to congregational management.[13] The reason this has been so widely accepted is precisely to be found in the fact that its underlying principles are also found quite overtly in the Christian scriptures. The very first page of the Bible describes people as being 'in God's image' (Genesis 1:26–7). Far from providing grounds for the indiscriminate exploitation of workers, that surely implies that people are special, and need to be handled with consideration and care. Moreover, other key documents of the Christian faith provide similarly distinctive models for the holistic environment in which women and men can achieve optimum maturity and self-fulfilment. This includes images of a harmonious ecological environment (Ephesians 1:10), as well as patterns for human relationships in which the social, racial and gender barriers so beloved of modernity are dismantled (Galatians 3:28). The New Testament's description of the new community as 'the body of Christ' is one of the most evocative symbols of systems thinking anywhere in the whole of literature (1 Corinthians 12:1–31). In the book to which we have already referred, Russell Ackoff highlights 'participative planning' as the management system for the new generation, and describes it as a process of 'encouraging and facilitating the participation of the others in the design of and planning for the organizations and institutions of which they are a part'. The way St Paul explains his concept of 'the body of Christ' – which is specifically related to his understanding of the character of the Christian God – must be one of the most striking examples of what Ackoff is advocating. It is certainly exceedingly difficult, if not impossible, to reconcile what the Bible actually promotes with the negative and destructive stereotypes of Christianity that are all too easily accepted.

Western Christians have not always lived up to this ideal, any more than industrial managers always reach their targets. I am not at all convinced that it is necessary to identify specifically religious roots for all the ailments of modern society. But insofar as the exploitation and alienation of workers has been based on underlying value systems, it makes more sense to trace that back to the materialist and mechanistic forms of belief that undermined the earlier Christian vision in the course of the Enlightenment, and which themselves were a direct product of the larger intellectual and social forces which also shaped European industrialization. If the church is implicated in some of the negative heritage of that period (and it is, as we shall see in our next chapter), the blame it must accept is in direct proportion to the extent to which it chose to abandon its own ideological roots in favour of the secular understandings promoted by the culture of modernity.

Moreover, there are questions to be raised about the simplistic assumption that disharmony in the workplace will be dispelled by the adoption of what is effectively a monistic belief system in which some sort of divine essence or life force runs through everything. This has to be seriously questioned purely on pragmatic grounds. For the practical outcome of that kind of worldview has consistently been a form of social stratification of the most extreme sort. On the Indian subcontinent, for example, where precisely this kind of outlook has dominated for centuries, it has produced the caste system, which is one of the most divisive, confrontational, fragmenting and personally degrading organizational structures imaginable. There is a profound inner inconsistency between the philosophical and religious foundation of what New Agers propose, and the proven practical outcome of it. Ackoff is right when he writes that our aspirations for the future will be 'based on important and fundamental beliefs, attitudes, and commitments', and that 'we cannot cope effectively with change unless we develop a better view of the world'.[14] But the proposed solution is hopelessly inadequate, and serves to draw attention once again to the serious ethical flaws of this worldview that we have already noted in previous chapters.

Personal Management

New Age concepts are not only being applied to provide a grand new philosophical underpinning for modern business. They are also being increasingly recommended to individuals as a way to overcome their own perceived inadequacies at a whole variety of levels. In the executive world, success is the only thing that counts. When New Age therapists give advice to their corporate clients, their message is that even the least successful manager can achieve absolutely anything he or she wants. Those who are apparent failures are the products of negative thinking, and achieve little because they have low expectations of themselves. The mind really is more real than matter, and by tuning in to cosmic wisdom, literally anyone can rise to the top. In the words of Marilyn Ferguson:

You can break through old limits, past inertia and fear, to levels of fulfilment that once seemed impossible ... to richness of choice, freedom, human closeness. You can be more productive, confident, comfortable with insecurity. Problems can be

*experienced as challenges, a chance for renewal, rather than
stress. Habitual defensiveness and worry can fall away.*[15]

This concept was popularized by Norman Vincent Peale through
his book *The Power of Positive Thinking*, and historically it has close
links to many of the nineteenth-century antecedents of the New
Age movement.[16] Managers all around the world have been
trained to begin each day with 'affirmations', in which they tell
themselves things like, 'I am a super salesperson, and grow every
day in every way', 'If it's going to be, it's up to me', or 'Imagination times vividness equals reality on the subconscious level.'

Like so much of what we have looked at here, it has just enough
truth in it to demand that we take it seriously. There can be no
denying that there are many depressed and defeated people around
in modern society. They are not just defeated, but defeatist. People
with a very poor self-image can easily convince themselves that they
are so unworthy and useless that any enterprise they get involved in
is doomed to failure before they even begin. The reasons for such
negative feelings are extremely diverse. Some start life with inbuilt
weaknesses, in physical or social skills. But many more have been
victimized and bullied by other people who have sought to use
them for their own selfish ends. Occasionally, their misery is com-
pounded by their own strongly held religious beliefs that encourage
them to believe they are terrible sinners, with whom God is angry,
and so there can be neither forgiveness nor recovery. Other promi-
nent elements in all this emotional baggage might also be poor
childhood memories, inadequate bonding with parents, guilt about
the past, and sexual hang-ups of one sort or another. All these
things can lead to repeated experiences of personal breakdown and
failure. Marilyn Ferguson is perfectly correct when she writes,
'High intention cannot coexist with a low self-image. Only those
who are awake, connected, and motivated can add to the synergy of
an organization.'[17]

Again, Christianity is often criticized as a major source of such problems. It cannot be denied that low self-esteem often goes hand in hand with certain forms of Christianity, not only the Roman Catholic tradition but also certain types of Calvinism and sectarian evangelicalism. Many people do find themselves put down because of the religious outlook of either other people or themselves – and we shall need to return to this issue in our final chapter. But whatever its origins, New Age personal management consultants offer an increasingly broad set of therapies to enable their clients to break out of this negative mindset. Once more, the advice on offer is frequently a variation on the familiar theme: we all choose to be who we are, and we are responsible for our successes and our failures. In order to make helpful choices we will need to deal with some blockage or imbalance in the flow of life-energy through our physical bodies, and thereby tune in more effectively to our inner spirit.

In 1987, William H. Kautz and Melanie Branon predicted that even activities such as the channelling of spirit guides would become commonplace in business education, and would be used more and more along with conventional methods.[18] That has already happened, and books written for busy executives have now progressed well beyond the themes of positive thinking, and are encouraging their readers to rely more and more on esoteric, and overtly 'spiritual' activities. Barrie Dolnick's book *The Executive Mystic* is typical of this genre. Its subtitle is 'Psychic Power Tools for Success', and by using these tools the author promises her readers a glittering future:

> *Psychic power tools ... can pave the way to a better, more productive workday and a more satisfying and successful career no matter what your field ... Psychic power tools will help you attract opportunity, maximize quality in yourself and others, counter negativity from colleagues, plan more effective meetings,*

make better hiring decisions, build more productive teams, and increase your ability to cut through the constant clutter and distraction around you.[19]

For those who may be hesitant, there is reassurance that this book is

not a ghost-busting guide for corporate [executives but rather] ... a completely accessible and practical guide to getting ahead in business using intuition and other psychic power sources ... using your psychic power will neither transform you into a late-blooming flower child nor turn you into an ardent New Ager.[20]

Nevertheless, in the process of explaining what 'psychic tools' are, and how they may be used to best effect, several familiar New Age themes recur. There is the all-pervasive suspicion of Enlightenment-inspired rationalism, as readers are advised in the preface that 'you must, to some degree, suspend your desire for logic and proof', reinforced in a later chapter by the advice to 'numb your mind'.[21] The search for personal self-understanding and the achievement of personal goals, even at the cost of perhaps persuading others to act against their own judgement, is another basic component:

Psychic power tools can be combined in many ways to bring about smooth business interactions and help you get what you want ... to help you influence even an unwilling audience ... [show you] how to combine your knowledge and skills to make a powerful impression.[22]

As aids to the pursuit of this satisfying and integrated lifestyle, readers are further advised about topics that include choosing office furniture, decorating work spaces, deciding what colour clothes to wear on different occasions, and how to defuse potentially confrontational situations. Much of this is homespun wisdom of the kind that previous generations might have taken for granted.

But there is a lot more than this to being a psychic executive. It is claimed that by using the techniques described here, readers can not only overcome their own weaknesses, but can actually change the shape of reality itself. This includes mind-over-matter things like trying to change your own personality by changing your handwriting,[23] but goes well beyond that with the claim that 'Psychic power is the ability to sense and see beyond physical reality, to remove the barrier of time and to shift or influence events accordingly'.[24] The author gives an example of such power when she describes how this practice of 'sending energy into the future' can not only open paths through traffic snarl-ups and create parking spaces where there were none, but also delay flight departures until the tuned-in executive is ready to board.[25]

Whether any individual can actually achieve this will depend on many factors. The heritage from past lives might have a bearing,[26] but more likely it will be related to the seriousness of purpose with which managers purify their space, build up their own good *karma*, are aware of their *chakras*, or know the astrological birth signs of other people in their organization. Crystals are powerful conductors of psychic energy, though they can be a mixed blessing, channelling negative energies as well as positive ones. But wisely used, they can make a significant difference to the spiritual atmosphere: 'Putting an amethyst next to your computer will help keep you feeling relaxed and at ease. Traveling with a clear quartz crystal can make a business trip seem like a breeze.'[27]

Colours can be used to similar effect, along with herbs and symbolic artefacts which might range from an acorn to a gargoyle, a candle, sand, shells or plants. The discovery of one's personal 'power animal' is of particular importance. This is the equivalent of a spirit guide, which is to be encountered in the context of a form of guided meditation, for which instructions are given. For those who find it hard to imagine a suitable beast, there is a long list of animals and their alleged secret powers.[28] Many other devices are also recommended, including the use of oracles to foresee future events, the Tarot, Runes, I Ching, and 'bibliomancy'.[29]

Those who are concerned about the negative influences that other colleagues might be creating should 'Sprinkle sea salt along the doorway or entryway to your workspace. This cleanses those who enter your environment.'[30] Other advice includes tuning in to the cycles of the moon, carrying various amulets and charms for different situations (there is a list of items that are especially powerful in different circumstances), instructions for 'a psychic practice called time shifting ... [which is] the ability to make time last "longer" when you need it to, and to make time pass more quickly when you can't wait anymore'.[31] Other proposals relate more directly to the success of business propositions:

> *If you are selling something, increase the desirability of your product by anointing it with an actual power scent ... or by creating a charm with the product's name written inside it.*
>
> *If you are trying to protect a certain project ... Sprinkle salt over it, then blow the salt off of it, into the wastebasket or out of the window.*
>
> *[When sending a project or proposal through the mail] You can pass a crystal over the project to increase its power ... Bless what you are sending out either aloud or with your exhaling breath.*[32]

The philosophical foundation for all this is something we have met several times before: the idea that we will get things right only by tuning in to cosmic powers beyond and greater than ourselves. Using the correct techniques will enable the individual to access the power behind the entire universe: 'Because psychic power is much bigger than your individual power – your psychic power is hooked up to the "cosmic hard drive" – you're endowed with the benefit of universal power, too.'[33]

We have already considered most of the questions raised by these practices, and it is unnecessary to rehearse them here. It is hard to know how seriously the average business manager regards all this, though the existence of a significant market for such books (and the courses that accompany them) suggests that more people are attracted to it than the average person in the street might imagine. But in some ways it is the underlying assumptions that are being made here about personal relationships that give most cause for concern. For lurking in the background here seems to be the belief that people have all chosen to be who and what they are, and if they are less successful than they wish, then they have only themselves to blame. Marilyn Ferguson quotes with approval an engineer who advised, 'Do things in the spirit of design research. Be willing to accept a mistake and redesign. There is no failure.'[34]

The view that ultimately there is neither good nor evil fits well with certain manifestations of the 'holistic' New Age outlook. It actually sits very uneasily alongside other New Age concerns for the environment, and the need for people to adopt simple lifestyles for the sake of the earth. But that is just one of the many inconsistencies and contradictions which characterize this whole amorphous movement. In terms of these management courses, the concern is focused on issues of practical morality. The assertion that we should all stand on our own two feet and take responsibility for our own lives can sound like the ultimate expression of personal freedom. It is easy to say that everyone should be free to make their own choices, and that we should all allow others to choose their own options, without necessarily embracing them ourselves. But having the freedom to choose is more complex than that. We all interact with other people, and our 'mistakes' can often have the most far-reaching impact on their personal possibilities. When individuals make choices solely on the ground of their own advantage, it can have disastrous knock-on effects for others in the wider community.

It is important here to emphasize the essentially syncretistic, New Age aspect of what is being promulgated in so-called spiritually oriented management courses. In theological terms, they are just another example of the way in which the New Age sucks up and uses materials from diverse religious traditions, while in the process introducing subtle transformations that demonstrate its essential nature as a creation of Western culture and undermine the principles of the traditions from which it has been derived. Bringing personal spirituality into the market-place is nothing new, and managers from many different religious traditions would automatically do this, because they see their faith commitments not as isolated aspects of their private lives, but as something that gives coherence to the whole of life. Significantly, when we examine a variety of world religions, we find a considerable degree of agreement on what would constitute an appropriate set of values within the work environment. For example, compassion and selfless service would be key concerns for managers motivated by the principles of Judaism, Christianity, Buddhism, and Hinduism.[35] The notion that some jobs are more appropriate than others would also be widely held (described by Buddhists as 'right livelihood', the principle that work should not involve suffering for people or animals), while almost all faiths have their own version of Martin Luther's notion that work itself is prayer. These values have little attraction to most people in postmodern Western culture, which tends to glorify the uncontrolled expression of individual desires. As a result, we find notions from many different religious traditions pulled from their original cultural contexts, and reduced to marketable techniques in order to fulfil the insatiable self-centredness of many of today's people. Far from being a new way for a new age, this is arguably an extension of one of the worst aspects of the old way of being. For the underlying philosophy is grounded not in any form of holistic mutuality, but is in reality a radical form of Enlightenment-inspired individualism. The disadvantaged and marginalized people of today's world are no strangers to this form of institutionalized selfishness, and morally it is hard to pay serious attention to an outlook that claims to be committed to a holistic world vision, but at the same time seemingly abandons any sense of social conscience. When this sort of belief about spirituality forms the core of some of the most popular managerial training programmes, it is little wonder that multinational corporations are often accused of being insensitive to the wider needs of the people they seek to serve.

Chapter Seven

What is the New Age
Saying to the Church?

Understanding the New Age can often seem a good deal more straightforward than trying to comprehend the church's response to it. Some Christians have embraced it uncritically, many more have condemned it without thinking, while others (perhaps the majority) are bemused and bewildered by the whole subject. This kind of reaction is fairly typical of the way the church has related to Western culture for at least the last three centuries, if not longer. Christians have not generally distinguished themselves as cultural innovators. They are more content to follow than to lead, often appearing to criticize movements they do not fully understand. Precisely because they do not understand them, all too often they have ended up arguing about peripheral matters while accepting the central tenets of the very movements of thought they profess to be opposed to. That happened in the nineteenth century with debates about Darwinism, it happened in the immediately preceding centuries with the unthinking acceptance of the mechanistic worldview of Enlightenment science, and even further back it happened in the days of the Roman empire when political power was mistakenly identified with spiritual power, and Greek philosophy was confused with the Christian Gospel.

This tendency of Christians to focus on minor details while missing the truly big issues is to be found in much recent thinking and writing about the New Age. By characterizing it as a disconnected and disjointed collection of more or less bizarre therapies and practices, it is not difficult to imagine that it can only be a passing fad. But the entire phenomenon deserves to be taken far more seriously than that. The fact that the church does not know how to engage with the New Age will not lead to its diminution. Whatever its weaknesses – and, as we have seen, there are many – the New Age is here to stay. Its strength is to be found in the fact that it has succeeded in identifying the questions that trouble the soul of all thinking people at the threshold of a new millennium. Whatever may be said about the answers that are on offer, there is no question that New Age people know the right questions, and they know how to address them in a way that captures the imagination of those who are disenchanted with the cultural status quo and are looking for a new way forward that will be not only intellectually credible, but also personally fulfilling. Unless the church develops a meaningful missiological engagement with the New Age outlook, then it is virtually certain that the steep decline of the church in the West will continue, while the new spirituality that will emerge to fill the vacuum will increasingly be constructed from materials that have very little Christian content in them. In fact, that is already happening. If you were to take everything that has been described in this book – not to mention the myriad of techniques and mythologies that have not featured at all – and ask, 'Who believes all this?', then the answer might easily be 'no one at all'. But if you take more general soundings about the various elements that go to make up the New Age worldview and ask, 'Who believes some of this?', then the outcome would be quite different. It is certainly likely that as the average person in the street tries to make sense out of life, the worldview they produce will have far more in common with New Age thinking than with anything remotely resembling mainstream Christianity. That does not necessarily make them New Agers in the narrow sense that they have interwoven all these elements to construct a consistent philosophical base. Very few people live on the basis of a self-consciously articulated ideology, anyway. Most simply pull together those things that help them to cope at particular points in life. For a variety of reasons, the things that people find helpful today are coming less from a Christian base and more from the popular spiritual nostrums of postmodern society.

Changing Beliefs and Christian Attitudes

One of the reasons why Christian options are less attractive today is related to the history of the West, and the part played in it by the church. A basic New Age assumption is that, if there is a way out of the mess, then traditional Western sources of spiritual guidance will be of no help in finding it. As we have already briefly noted in our first chapter, the church is perceived as a part of the old cultural establishment that actually created the present predicament. Consequently, it is so tainted by inadequate and unsatisfactory metaphysical understandings that it is by definition incapable of exercising any constructive role in charting a new course for the future. Most people have no difficulty in drawing a straight line from the Enlightenment to the church, and when one part of the cultural edifice begins to crumble, that inevitably places major question-marks against all its other central components. The conclusion is that if Christianity is part of the problem, it cannot also be part of the solution. Consequently, the only place to find useful guidance as we move into a new millennium will be in other cultures and worldviews, or within ourselves.

Christians may reasonably protest that this is not an altogether fair understanding of history. It is no doubt true that the church has been blamed for many of the mistakes of Western imperialism – whether in science, education or colonization – when it was, at most, an unwilling partner. But it is now equally clear that Christians of previous generations bought into the Enlightenment vision quite uncritically, and as a result their successors are now paying the price. The real driving force behind the New Age is growing dissatisfaction with the cultural heritage of the West, and insofar as Western culture has – empirically at least – been Christian culture, dissatisfaction with Christianity is inevitably going to be a significant element within that. This may seem to be a harsh and undifferentiated judgement on Christian history. It is, and if this was a study of the interaction between church and culture over the past several centuries, it would need to be qualified and defined with much greater care. There are many subtle nuances in the church's relationship with recent Western history, for individual Christians have made a considerable positive contribution to the evolution of the kind of open, democratic social and political systems we now enjoy – and which, ironically, have made possible such strident criticism of the church's track record. But from a missiological perspective, the central question is not whether the negative perceptions of the church's role in the development of modernity are all true in the absolute sense, but whether these impressions are widely believed to be true. On the whole, I believe they are, and acceptance of that fact will need to be the starting point for a Christian engagement with the New Age outlook. It will sometimes be appropriate to set the record straight, and point out that Christians have not single-handedly been responsible for everything that has gone wrong in the world, as some critics have been inclined to suppose. But missiologically that should not be the first response. For Christians have done plenty for which they now bear corporate guilt, and repentance will often be the most appropriate way to deal with that. Attempting to rewrite history will not work, nor will it be convincing to claim that the church did certain things because it had lost touch with its biblical roots. That may well be true in some cases, and that fact alone ought to challenge today's Christians constantly to ask whether what we now see as 'Christian' values are indeed derived from the biblical tradition, or whether, like generations before us, we are not merely following the fads and fancies of our own rather different cultural context. But that is a debate that needs to go on internally, within the church. In terms of the church's mission among New Agers, that kind of approach sounds too much like special pleading and self-justification. Moreover, the way the church now interacts with the New Age is not simply a matter of theoretical apologetics, but will be central to the church's mission. For it is a simple fact that those most attracted to the New Age are, in sociological terms, the people who in the past formed the natural constituency of the churches.[1]

Considering the way in which the New Age has raised these questions – not to mention the way its emergence has opened up the whole subject of spirituality and placed it firmly on the popular agenda – one might have expected that the church would have paid more attention to it. There have, of course, been many books on the topic written by Christians, mostly in opposition to the New Age message. But in a scathing dismissal of such books, religion professor Irving Hexham accuses Christian writers of approaching the topic 'in a simplistic style ... characterized by reductionism, lack of definition, and poor scholarship'. Even worse: some either 'deliberately distort their evidence or do not know how to read a text'.[2] That is a damning criticism, especially from a scholar who identifies himself as being an evangelical Christian. It is, however, overstated, and while I recognize some of the trends to which he draws attention, the range of Christian responses to New Age thinking is in fact more diverse and sophisticated than he indicates. By highlighting the work of a few extremists, he sets up an easy target for himself. Ironically, this procedure is not unlike the very people he criticizes, for they too tend to focus on some of the more bizarre manifestations of the New Age, which is precisely why they then adopt a simplistic analysis, seeing it as a collection of disparate and unconnected practices rather than a major spiritual force within the cultural change to postmodernity.

It cannot be denied, though, that those Christians who have sought to engage with the New Age have not always been as perceptive as they should have been. They have made two mistakes in particular which have tended to undermine, rather than enhance, the Christian case.

First has been the tendency to adopt an uncritical approach which assumes that the New Age is some kind of monolithic movement that can be categorized rather easily. This is a natural model for Christians to adopt, for it is based on the organizational structure of the church itself, particularly in the period of Christendom. But as we have seen, the entire nature of the New Age is quite different from this. Unfortunately, this undifferentiated approach has led some Christians to perceive the New Age as an organized conspiracy, determined to undermine Western civilization as we know it.[3]

They see it as a monstrous threat – even at times relating it to an underground resurgence of the Nazi movement – and talk of arming themselves for a spiritual confrontation of massive proportions. They have convinced themselves that if the last great battle of Armageddon is not actually the engagement of Christianity and the New Age, then there is some subtle connection between them, for the New Age and its leaders are being characterized as demonic and Satanic – even perhaps the Antichrist. But if Western civilization is collapsing, it is not as a result of any New Age conspiracy against it, but because of inherent flaws in its own ideological base.

Indeed, the New Age – however inadequately – is trying to ask where we go from here, given that the Western Enlightenment vision is no longer viable. I have been unable to find any significant evidence of a New Age conspiracy to undermine society. On those occasions when I have heard somewhat triumphalist language used to describe the New Age future, it has struck me as little different from the way Christians speak when they similarly claim that they will 'revolutionize the world with the Gospel'.

More seriously, Christians fail to listen carefully to what is actually being said within the New Age. For example, it is widely taken for granted that the New Age has one consistent worldview, that can best be described as monistic. However, as earlier chapters have demonstrated, that is only part of the picture, for there is also a clearly dualistic aspect to much New Age thinking.[4] The apparent inconsistency of New Age 'theology' has been a major reason why some commentators have dismissed the entire movement as irrational and nonsensical. But a more productive understanding will locate these apparent contradictions in the New Age's foundational understanding of the nature of human alienation. For the experienced alienation of Western people today is not, on the whole, a cosmological or metaphysical phenomenon, but a cultural alienation. In this context, the ultimate expression of spiritual ignorance is critical scientific thinking, and it is from this that the human spirit must be set free.

This is an area in which Christians have few models to inform their approach, which no doubt explains why virtually all Christian responses to the New Age fall back on the security of what look like tried and tested apologetic approaches, rooted in rational analysis. It is not that the New Age ought not to be subjected to such criticism. Indeed, in the face of the emergence of an increasingly irrational postmodern intellectual elite in our universities, one of the things that Christians perhaps need to bear witness to today is the fact that humans are creatures of reason.

Notwithstanding all the mistakes that previous generations undoubtedly made, the capacity for rational understanding is one of the fundamental marks of being fully human. But to engage with the New Age only at this level is a serious mistake. For to most New Agers, this methodology is one of the key contributory factors to the crisis in Western culture. Using the tools of modernity to address the New Age will get nowhere, for it is by definition immune to rational criticism. Indeed, having the courage to transcend the boundaries of conventional linear Western forms of perception, and to discard the narrow confines of an over-reliance on rationalism is, for many, the ultimate expression of the kind of spirituality that will take us forward into the future. Psychology professor Marilyn Ferguson expresses it eloquently:

> *We live what we know. If we believe the universe and ourselves to be mechanical, we will live mechanically. On the other hand, if we know that we are part of an open universe, and that our minds are a matrix of reality, we will live more creatively and powerfully.*[5]

We are on surer ground when we draw attention to the moral relativism of much that is in the New Age. But in the process of making an honest assessment of the flaws in the New Age, Christians also need to be prepared to face up to the weaknesses of the church itself. The simple fact is that, while many aspects of the New Age prescription for the ailments of today's world may be nonsensical and meaningless, its diagnosis of the disease is too accurate for comfort. Dean W.R. Inge (1860–1954) is reputed to have observed that 'A church that is married to the spirit of its age will find itself widowed in the next', and that just about sums up where Christians today find themselves. Christian beliefs, spirituality and lifestyles have become almost exclusively focused on rational systems of thinking, with a consequent marginalization of the intuitional, the emotional, the relational and the spiritual.[6]

There is a need to recognize those things that are right about the New Age analysis. At the forefront of that would be the opinion that we have all been influenced by the optimistic rationalist-materialism of recent Western culture, as a result of which our capacity for spiritual perception has been dimmed, if not totally extinguished. In that sense, we are all victims of our cultural heritage. To talk of Christianity and the New Age in terms of 'us' and 'them' is to miss one of the most fundamental points of all. The Christian Gospel has always maintained that the world needs to be reinvented, and the reimagining of how life might be – how God intends it to be – is at the heart of the teaching of Jesus. The church has not always pushed that vision forward. But now that the legacy of secularism is being so thoroughly questioned, if not rejected, many others who have never regarded themselves as within the Christian orbit are asking the very same questions about the meaning of life and the possibilities for the future. Moreover, there is considerable overlap between the questions I hear being asked in New Age circles, and those being raised by concerned Christians. Christians right across the ecclesiastical and theological spectrum have been criticized by other Christians for engaging in practices that their opponents claim belong to the New Age.

Throughout the 1980s, British church leaders were criticized for their involvement in services relating to environmental and inter-faith concerns. The World Council of Churches was attacked by conservative groups for its programme on Justice, Peace and the Integrity of Creation. The 'alternative ministry' of St James's Church of England, in London's Piccadilly, has been condemned as being a major breeding ground for New Age views. Meanwhile, those conservative Christians who have gone on the offensive over these matters have often engaged in behaviour that would be perfectly at home in the context of New Age therapies, while much

New Age speculation about spirit guides and extra-terrestrials looks positively tame when placed alongside the detailed knowledge of the activity of demons and other spirits that is being claimed by some contemporary Christians.[7] Anyone familiar with the Christian scene today – especially the evangelical wing – cannot fail to notice the huge increase in the popularity of motivational seminars and workshops, which constantly extol the virtues of the power of the mind and will over material reality, and suggest that with enough faith their clients can change anything. Moreover, the tensions themselves are not just symptomatic of the historic divergence between conservative and more liberal Christians. Within the conservative evangelical constituency, the debate about so-called 'post-evangelicalism' is a variation on the same theme, while in the Roman Catholic tradition the controversy surrounding the expulsion of Matthew Fox from the Dominican Order also focused on very similar issues.[8] Meanwhile, growing numbers of ordinary church members who are often unaware of these arguments intuitively follow the free-market philosophy of our day, and choose their spiritual diet from a variety of sources: church on Sunday, then the rest of the week depending on things like yoga meditation for self-awareness, and consultations with extra-terrestrial entities for guidance on major life decisions. Some leading practitioners of what are regularly labelled New Age therapies are, in the remainder of their lives, evangelical Christians, and cannot understand what the fuss is all about.

Christians should hardly be surprised by this degree of overlap between questions now being raised within the church, and the concerns of the wider culture. This is exactly what might be expected in the light of any sort of doctrine of creation or incarnation based on the biblical understanding that people are made 'in God's image'. The examples just mentioned highlight the fact that the debate between Christians and others – and within the Christian tradition – is less about the nature of the questions, and more concerned with the kind of answers that might be found helpful. In particular, knowing where to draw appropriate boundaries has become a major problem area. If New Agers tend to dismiss Christianity because of their preconceived understandings, then Christians can also be inclined to do little more than repeat their own inherited prejudices. A key challenge for Christians is to be open enough to acknowledge the source of some of these prejudices, or presuppositions. For one of the dangers faced by the church in seeking to engage with the New Age spiritual search is that it will present itself as an apologist not for the Gospel, but for the mindset and worldview of modernity.[9]

There need be no uncertainty about my own preferred starting point here. However it may be expressed, the Gospel is only the Gospel if it is clearly continuous with the values and beliefs communicated by Jesus. Within that, I mean to include not only the actual teachings attributed to Jesus in the New Testament, but also Jesus' lifestyle and attitudes as we find them in the Gospels, and the beliefs to which his death, resurrection and the experience of the Holy Spirit gave rise among the first generation of his disciples. But the sting in the tail here is that, if I am correct in thinking that the church has largely perpetuated the values of an essentially non-spiritual culture (the Enlightenment), then the assumptions many of us have about Jesus (and his early followers) are likely to have been formed not directly by the biblical tradition itself, but by the intellectual framework through which we have received it. This in turn goes well beyond the Enlightenment in the narrow sense, for it also entails a critical awareness of the way in which the philosophical models of ancient Greece have influenced – and in some cases corrupted – the ways in which the Gospel has been understood. The new questions being raised today are in fact highlighting some very important issues that have a clear biblical mandate, but which have often been overlooked in the past because of cultural constraints. Far from being a negative influence, the insistent way in which the New Age has cast doubt upon the received wisdom of Western culture is providing a new perspective from which Christians need to look afresh at the Bible, with the expectation that they will discover truths that have always been there, but have been overlooked because of our love affair with the culture of modernity. Moreover, it seems to me that this procedure itself has a biblical antecedent in the way Luke depicts Paul's sharing of the Christian message in Athens – using the spiritual search of the (clearly non-Christian) culture to highlight aspects of Christian faith that otherwise might remain hidden. Of course, there are two possible dangers in this. One is that we lose sight of the biblical message, and the other is that we make the same mistakes as our forebears. It will be no more profitable in the long run to identify the Gospel with the values of postmodernity and the New Age than it has been to confuse it with modernity and the Enlightenment. But there will always be a risk factor in any missiological engagement with culture, and to be aware of this is perhaps the best safeguard against making Christianity into what we would like it to be, rather than allowing ourselves to hear the Gospel, stand under its judgement, and respond in creative ways to its challenge.

Challenging the Church

In 1993, the now infamous Re-Imagining Conference took place in Minneapolis, attended by over two thousand delegates and sponsored by all the mainline denominations in the USA, together with other para-church organizations. It was part of the American observance of the Ecumenical Decade in Solidarity with Women, inaugurated by the World Council of Churches for the ten-year period 1988–98. This conference engendered one of the most acrimonious debates ever seen among American Christians, mainly concerned with the worship that took place, and in particular its adoption of female images to describe both God and Christian experience, which to some appeared little more than a form of neo-paganism dressed up in biblical terminology. It is neither appropriate nor necessary to divert here from our main theme in order to give further consideration to that event and its continuing fallout. Whatever its failings, no one ought to disagree with the idea that the Gospel now needs to be 'reimagined' for this generation and this changing culture. The Gospel has always needed to be presented in terms that can be understood by different cultures, while remaining true to its roots. Christians in the non-Western world have long been familiar with the notion of 'contextualization'. Contemporary missions scholars sometimes give the impression that this was a new insight discovered in the mid-twentieth century. In reality, Christians of all generations have practised it. The existence of four Gospels in the New Testament, instead of just one, is directly related to the need of the earliest Christians to make their message accessible to people with different religious experiences and concerns. In the book of Acts, Luke depicts early preachers like Paul adopting different strategies in different cities, so that the Hebrew scriptures would be central in speaking to Jews (e.g. Acts 13:15–42), while Greek poets were favoured in Athens (Acts 17:16–31), and a more discursive interactive style prevailed in the Hall of Tyrannus at Ephesus (Acts 19:9–10). The Church Fathers recast the Gospel into the mould of Greek philosophy to try and communicate it more effectively to the people whom they met. To use today's jargon, they were all trying to 'reimagine' the Gospel for their own circumstances. They all also knew there would be a thin line between contextualizing the message into the culture and allowing the culture to alter the agenda. Even Paul was alternatively criticized for being too Jewish or not Jewish enough! To stay the same, the Gospel must be changing all the time, for the language of yesterday will not necessarily convey the same meaning today as it did in its original context.

The emergence of the New Age has actually helped to create an atmosphere of spiritual openness within which Christians ought to find it easy to share their faith. The overwhelming majority of people who get involved in New Age spirituality are engaged in a serious search for God. If anything, they are likely to be more open to a radical life-changing encounter than are many Christians. Furthermore, the New Age agenda has many striking points of contact with the agenda of the Gospel. Concern for personal freedom and maturity, for the environment, for peace and justice, for self-discovery, for a holistic view of life – these are all things that were an integral part of the message of Jesus. The most significant difference between Christian faith and New Age spirituality is not to be found in their social, economic, political or environmental hopes and aspirations, but in their beliefs about how these goals are likely to be achieved. Whereas the New Age outlook typically identifies the basic dilemma as an alienated or undeveloped consciousness, Christians take evil and suffering seriously, and affirm that the underlying problem is a moral one, not a metaphysical one. They recognize the reality of undeserved suffering, and the presence of objective evil in the world. Further, while the New Age in all its manifestations is fiercely individualistic, the Gospel claims that salvation is rooted in communitarian concerns, and that the improvement of one's interior, personal life is not the primary goal of the spiritual search, but is one outcome of the rediscovery of the meaning of true community. In addition, Christians will part company with those New Agers who claim that we are all God, or all equal with God (though they will also be aware that not all New Agers believe this anyway). They will suggest that 'going within' is unlikely by itself to solve all our problems. Indeed, they will want to argue that an over-reliance on our own resources might well have been a prime cause of most of our recent difficulties. And they will insist that there is an objectivity about the way the world is that requires us to pay attention to the discovery of absolute values and beliefs, rather than relying on what seems 'right for you'.

Having said that, however, we need to recognize that over the centuries the effective contextualization of the Gospel has not only required that the Christian message be translated, as it were, into the thought forms and idioms of the day. At particular times and places, specific aspects of the Christian message have also emerged as more relevant to the needs of different generations, as a consequence of which they have been emphasized more than other aspects. So, for example, in the Middle Ages the suffering brought to entire populations by outbreaks of plague were a major social scourge – and so much religious art of the period highlighted the sufferings of Christ, often in a grotesque way, but making the point that God also had suffered. In fifteenth-century Europe, personal guilt and the need for forgiveness was a major issue for many people, and one reason the Protestant Reformers made such an impact was because they addressed that question so effectively. In the Victorian era, there was a major concern with death and the hereafter – and the effective evangelists of that generation were the ones who dealt with that issue. From the perspective of today, their sermons and hymns often seem sentimental and overpious, because our primary concerns are different. As the church has spread into the non-Western world, it has been important to explore what the Gospel has to say about matters of fairness and justice.

In this process, not only has the Christian faith been shared, but it has also on significant occasions been reshaped. It is not so long ago that virtually all Western Christians took it for granted that slavery was part of the biblical vision. Some of the fiercest opponents of the US civil rights movement, led so eloquently by Baptist pastor Dr Martin Luther King Jr, were other Christians. Because it ran contrary to their own preconceptions about the Bible's message, they not only questioned the reality of his own faith but they accused him of undermining the whole of the Christian cause. Twenty years later, the very same arguments were being revisited in South Africa. The institution of apartheid was, in effect, the projection into politics of a particular understanding of the Bible and its message – and it was opposed by other Christians, inspired by the same Bible. Not only is it the case that certain aspects of the Gospel will be especially relevant to particular situations, but it is also true that new questions raised in different generations do lead to the discovery of insights that were always there in the Bible, but which for a variety of reasons had been sidelined or ignored. In this light, Christians ought to be able to approach the key questions of today's generation, not only with the confidence that the Gospel will have something relevant to say, but also with the expectation that their own prior understandings of faith might well be challenged in the process. If the Gospel stands in judgement over all of humanity – Christians included – they should not expect any less.

The Gospel in the New Age

This is not the place to spell out in great detail what a reimagination of the Gospel for the New Age might look like. I have already made a start on that in other recent writings, and will continue to do so elsewhere.[10] What I propose to do here is to set up a series of signposts which will, I hope, point in some appropriate directions and suggest further avenues to be explored. I have grouped these under different headings below, but mostly for convenience and to make the book easier to read. In reality, they are all interconnected, and are different facets of what is in effect the same fundamental question.

The Rational and the Emotional

Given that the New Age is, in effect, the religious manifestation of postmodernity, it will surprise no one that it is characterized by a serious mistrust, if not outright rejection, of rationality. G.K. Chesterton is reputed to have once remarked that 'When people cease to believe in God, they do not believe in nothing, they believe in anything.' This is an appropriate comment, not only on much that is going on under the guise of the New Age, but on postmodernity more widely. There are good reasons for questioning the rationalistic attitude that has dominated much recent Western thinking, but it is a mistake if, in the process, rationality itself is rejected. By rationalistic I mean the outlook which says there is nothing worth knowing that cannot be discerned purely by human thought processes. That assumption has led to the development of a fragmented, reductionist way of understanding human nature, and deserves to be discarded. Many New Agers have reacted against this in such an extreme fashion that it seems they automatically distrust anything that makes logical ('left-brained') sense. Bhagwan Shree Rajneesh has claimed that rational, analytical thinking will actually prevent a person from achieving spiritual enlightenment: 'It is not that the intellect sometimes misunderstands. Rather, the intellect always misunderstands. It is not that the intellect sometimes errs; it is that the intellect is the error.'[11]

Influenced by such notions, increasing numbers of people assume that if something seems to make sense by our normal definitions of logic, it must automatically be suspect. They live their lives on the basis of information supplied to them through fairies and elves, dolphins and crystals, and techniques such as self-hypnosis and channelling, encouraged by the success of TV programmes like *The X-Files*, which make it all look realistic. The most charitable comment one can make is that these channelled messages are of uncertain origin, and therefore cannot be tested or authenticated in any meaningful sense. Yet it is frequently claimed that Jesus himself was some kind of channeller of spirit guides, and that various Gnostic gospels provide evidence for that, while the New Testament as we know it is dismissed as an unbelievable hoax concocted in the fourth century by nasty male church leaders, to keep women in subjection, to affirm their own domination, and to rid the Christian tradition of unacceptable concepts such as reincarnation. Of course, there is absolutely no evidence at all in support of any of this, but that has not prevented the popular media from adopting it as almost their standard understanding of the Christian tradition.

This rejection of rationality also surfaces, as we have seen, in the way in which Christianity is discredited by the insistence on a one-sided view of history in which Christians are portrayed as being the cause of the environmental crisis, or the instigators of all the world's war and injustice. To suggest that this is the natural and inevitable outcome of following Jesus is mischievous and untrue. It simply draws attention to the fact that Christians, like everyone else, frequently make wrong moral choices. Alongside all this, New Agers continue to perpetuate their own mythologies quite uncritically. Much of what is handed on in New Age circles is simply nonsensical. Shirley Maclaine quotes the well-known channeller Kevin Ryerson asking, 'Did what came through *feel* right? They've told me to just trust my feelings. There's nothing else you can do once you begin to ask these questions.'[12]

A few pages later she adds, 'The thing is it all seems to be about "feeling", not thinking.'[13] Recent Western culture has often preferred reason over emotion and feelings. But feelings by themselves are unlikely to be any more useful than rationality by itself. We need a more holistic paradigm that takes into account all the different ways in which we can 'know' things or people. To rely on feelings to the exclusion of reason is merely perpetuating the very same reductionist attitudes that New Agers claim to dislike so much. To be fully human requires that feelings and reason work together in harmony.

Having said that, however, it is undeniable that Christianity has tended to be much happier with reason than with emotion. The precise extent to which faith and feelings have been divorced from one another varies between different denominational traditions. But it is generally true that, to cope with church, people need to be able to process abstract concepts through their mental processes, and those who more naturally deal with things in an intuitive, artistic or creative way will find little that speaks to them. Most Christians have tended to prefer the propositional way of articulating truth, and express varying degrees of uneasiness not only with the imagination, but with other non-cognitive things such as images and symbols. In contrast, Jesus (repeating teaching from the Hebrew tradition) promoted a holistic image of disciple-ship when he spoke of responding to God with 'heart, soul, mind and strength' (Mark 12:30, quoting Deuteronomy 6:4–5).

Personal Growth

The longing for wholeness is one of the most widely felt human needs today. In terms of contextualizing the Gospel in contempo-rary culture, the development of a relevant theology of the human person and of meaningful models of spiritual growth is probably the most important aspect of all. People feel disjointed, out of tune with their physical environment, out of touch with other peo-ple, and even unable to come to terms with themselves. There is a lot of hurt around, and many wounded people who are looking for personal healing. To be relevant to life in the next millennium, any religious faith will have to be capable of dealing effectively with such feelings of alienation and lostness.

This should hardly be a challenge for the Christian message. Jesus himself offered to make people whole, and throughout his teaching he described a life of fulfilment in which the divisions that cause pain can be healed. A holistic lifestyle features strongly on the pages of the New Testament. It is God's will. Yet the Christian church is one of the most striking examples not of wholeness, but of separation. Most people have just a few images that will live with us throughout our lives. One of mine is a TV news report of the 1991 Gulf War, which showed soldiers standing in the desert celebrating the Christian Eucharist. They had two tables set up alongside each other, one for Protestants, the other for Roman Catholics. They could live – and die – together, but not worship together! This sort of thing hardly commends the Christian faith to genuine searchers after the life of the spirit. It only serves to reinforce the negative and destructive image of the church that they already have.

Local congregations can probably do little to address big issues of that sort. But the insidious persistence of a kind of closet Christianity is found in parishes of all denominations. To many church members, Christian faith seems to be only an optional extra in life, to be worn on Sundays to go to church and then discarded for the rest of the week. The lack of deep connection between Christian values and the lifestyles actually adopted by Christian people is not only contrary to the teaching of Jesus and the example of the first disciples, it also has no appeal to those who are searching for a more integrated way of being. Anyone looking for a holistic answer to life's challenges will quite likely find the church to be too bland and undemanding. The days when people's needs for personal identity could be met through shallow relationships and glib moralistic advice have gone for ever.

Shirley Maclaine helpfully identifies this sense of searching for a deeper reality when she describes a British politician with whom she once had a relationship. In writing of this man, whom she calls Jerry, she says:

*He had travelled through Africa as a young man. But when he
spoke of it, I suddenly realized that he never once mentioned
what he ate, what he touched, what he saw, what he smelled, how
he felt. He spoke mainly about Africa as a sociological trip, not
as a human trip. He spoke of how the 'masses' were exploited
and poor and colonized, but never how they really lived and felt
about it.*[14]

With only a few changes in terminology, that accurately describes
how many Christians think of their faith. It is a sociological (theological) trip, not a human trip. This is largely due to the way Christian theology – both liberal and conservative – has allowed
rationalism to evacuate it of any sense of direct encounter with
God. But on the level of personal formation, Ian Wray speaks for
many when he complains that Christianity has a 'traditional lack of
therapeutic, by which I mean the lack of any real body of ideas and
practices to help people change'. He goes on to observe that 'the
near total absence of practical aids to human psychological and
spiritual growth within Christianity left a vacuum which psychotherapy had to fill, based upon principles which it had to
discover for itself'.[15]

It is certainly the experience of many people that, when they
encounter Christianity, they are more likely to be put down than
to be lifted up. This is one of the points at which the New Age
critique has raised questions that demand an answer. Why do so
many Christians suffer from a low sense of self-esteem, overbur-
dened with a sense of guilt and feelings of personal worthlessness?
The New Age answer to such problems is to affirm the power of
positive thinking, and to suggest that 'You are what you make
yourself'. We have already noted the moral inadequacy of that
outlook, and in particular its inability to deal with the reality of
evil. Christians invariably have a more robust attitude to the presence of sin in the world, but have regularly made the mistake of

understanding sin in purely personal terms. This was a natural thing for Western Christians to do, influenced by the individualism of the Enlightenment outlook. From that vantage point, it has then been easy for notions of 'sin' to be used as a form of social stratification through which the church has become judgemental about people who are not a part of its own structures. This kind of unbiblical dualism has not only created a great deal of misery, it has also encouraged the acceptance of a shallow and theologically deviant understanding of both sin and salvation. In biblical terms, sin is not a purely individual phenomenon. On the contrary, it has a universal character that encompasses the breakdown of all relationships, not only between people themselves, but between people and the natural environment as well as between people and God. Whatever else may be said about him (and I am by no means uncritical of many of his ideas), Matthew Fox has done a great service to the church in drawing attention to these questions. They will not go away.[16]

A related challenge is how to deal with the church's love of hierarchies. To a greater extent than most Christians would like to acknowledge, the inherited organizational and theological styles find their roots in the patriarchal culture of the European imperialism (and, beyond that, back to ancient Rome). When imperialist expansion was high on the agenda of Western nations – whether at the time of the Crusades or the conquest of South America, or in the creation of the British empire – our forebears needed an imperialistic God, and the church was not slow to supply the need. All too often, 'salvation' for the non-Western world was the sharp end of a sword. This overemphasis on just one aspect of the biblical picture of God (transcendence) has left the church in a weak position when it comes to showing how the Gospel relates to the rather different concerns of today's people, who on the whole are rejecting such images of 'power over' others, in favour of a more relational style of 'power in partnership with' others. When one recalls that at the heart of the Gospel is not a God who became an all-conquering monarch, but a God who became a child, the perpetuation of overt images of top-down power is not merely culturally questionable, but theologically heretical. Though the Bible has its fair share of transcendent images, it also insists that Jesus is the most perfect revelation of the character of God, and in the process redefines who God is, in terms of weakness, vulnerability and powerlessness. That image has been marginalized, for a variety of reasons. One has to do with the political power of the church in the period of Christendom. Another is the unhealthy domination of Christian thinking by the uncritical adoption of a view of 'God' derived from Greek philosophy, in which all our theological outcomes need to be 'successful', and there is little or no space for tragedy and suffering, or for emotions like grief and failure. For people struggling to come to terms with the flaws in life, a God who is remote and 'successful' seems irrelevant. A God who understands suffering, and is able to accept failure while empowering those who are broken to move forward into new life, will speak more powerfully to today's people. In reality, this second image of God is absolutely central to the New Testament. But by creating the impression that the Gospel is actually about the first, Christians can prevent spiritual searchers from effectively hearing what the Gospel might have to say.

Another feature of church life stemming from the same source is a deep-seated unwillingness to allow – still less empower – those who are not the 'right' people to have any influence. This frequently expresses itself in a patriarchal form, as the contributions of women are marginalized and rejected, and overt images of maleness are continually projected as intrinsic to Christian faith – whether in the words of hymns or the insistent use of exclusively male imagery for God, despite the fact that none of that is intrinsic to the Bible itself.[17] We have already examined Russell Ackoff's vivid descriptions of the outmoded and useless models of the Machine Age, in which *employees were treated as replaceable machines or machine parts even though they were known to be human beings. Their personal objectives ... were considered irrelevant by employers ... the very simple repetitive tasks they were given to do were designed as though they were to be performed by machines.*[18]

In discussing New Age management courses, it was strongly argued that the New Testament projects a very different model of organizational structure. Yet the truth of the matter is that Ackoff's description fits the churches too closely for comfort. There are hundreds of thousands of congregations where the members are only cogs in an ecclesiastical machine run by other people. The simple truth is that here, as elsewhere, the church has been all too eager to adopt the secular standards and practices of the prevailing culture. As a result, when people look at Christians, they often see more of the hierarchies and bureaucracies that they struggle with elsewhere, and they know intuitively that this is not where they will find personal spiritual fulfilment. One of the key characteristics of our age is people's desire to construct their own ways of understanding and responding to God, in the context of their own personal search for spiritual wholeness. In describing the kind of organizations to which people will be attracted, Ackoff counsels that

What is required is that individuals be able to evaluate their own quality of life, that they have an opportunity to improve it, that they be encouraged to do so, and that their efforts to do so be facilitated ... [this will be brought about] by encouraging and facilitating the participation of the others in the design of and planning for the organizations and institutions of which they are a part.[19]

As before, a striking example of all that is to be found in the New Testament, this time in the life of Jesus. One of the major distinguishing marks of the way he called people into discipleship was his insistence that he would create the infrastructure of spirituality, not its super-structure. He then left his disciples to work out for themselves how and what to build on that infrastructure. Discipleship became their responsibility, not his, and facing that responsibility was, for them, a major component of what gave life its spiritual meaning.[20] That is the kind of context in which personal growth can take place.

The top-down style of being church rarely finds it possible to offer people effective solutions to their problems. It is easy enough to talk about matters such as God's grace and forgiveness. But if the church only diagnoses the problems, without offering effective solutions, that is a very dangerous psychological and spiritual game. As the New Age has shown, people are looking for hands-on therapies. It simply will not do for solutions to be offered only in a theoretical sort of way. Knowing that there is an escape from guilt and failure is going to be of little practical assistance, if people then have to access it themselves without really knowing what is being recommended or required. Western people (the British more than most) love to keep themselves private. But leaving peo-ple to work out the implications of faith for themselves – just them and God in a secret place – is little more than a subtle adaptation of the essentially secular gospel of Western individualism, the spir-itual equivalent of the economic exhortation to 'stand on your own two feet'. If the Holy Spirit offers the prospect of power to change – as the New Testament states clearly on every page – then the next question is, 'How do I access that power?' For that, rather more than theological statements will be required, however true they might be. There is a need for spiritual disciplines, techniques and practices that will facilitate people in relating to their own inner selves, while consciously and deliberately opening their lives to God's presence, in order to effect radical change. There is also a need for a more playful spirituality. Though it is often argued that the decline of the churches is related to their having become middle-class institutions, a more likely cause is to be located in the inability of the church to appeal to those who have more intuitive and artistic ways of being. Paradoxically, there is a whole rich Christian tradition of interactive and affective (essentially non-cognitive) spirituality which had been marginalized and largely ignored until New Agers came along and began to ransack it for their own purposes. People need something tangible through which to express their deepest life commitments. But in order to explore them effectively, they need safe spaces. The creation of such spaces should be a top priority for the church – not only because it will assist the contextualization of the Gospel in contemporary culture, but also because it is a way of being that is quite fundamental and central to the teaching of the New Testament.

The Mystical, the Numinous, and the Supernatural

Mention of spiritual disciplines moves us on to another major area of embarrassment for many Christians when dealing with the New Age. Not all New Agers have a strong belief in some kind of spiritual reality lying beyond this world, but probably the majority do. Over and above that, the whole question of direct personal perception of the divine is, in varying ways, of growing importance to an increasing proportion of the population. The precise way in which this is described seems less important than how Christians will relate to it, which is why I am happy to use words like mystical, numinous, supernatural – or even spiritual – as more or less interchangeable.

Discovering what Christians think about any of this is not straightforward, and the uneasiness that is displayed when such matters are raised readily convinces New Agers that the church is so thoroughly locked into a rationalist-materialist thought pattern that, at best, its opinions are irrelevant, and at worst, probably most Christians either have no belief in this sort of thing or have no idea what to believe.

I remember a conversation with one of the world's leading New Agers, who had been raised as a Christian in the Baptist tradition, and had a shrewd understanding of the typical Christian mind-set. Explaining to me why, for her, New Age made more sense than the church, she highlighted what for her was a meaningless contradiction: 'The church is full of rationalists. I know Christians who would fight to the death to defend the belief that Jesus performed miracles, but then will fight just as vigorously to deny that there is any such thing as the miraculous in today's world.' She was describing the classic reformed evangelical position, which to her was basically a rationalist viewpoint with an unexpected twist in it: the supernatural is all right, so long as it is firmly in the past and has no immediate connection to life here and now. That made no sense to her, not only because she herself had had many mystical experiences, but also because she found this sense of the numinous almost everywhere in the Bible. In addition to the stories about Jesus, she highlighted Moses' experience at the burning bush (Exodus 3:1–14), Elijah's experience of the 'still small voice' (1 Kings 19:3–18), Ezekiel being mystically transported from Babylon to Jerusalem and back in what seemed to her like astral projection (Ezekiel 8:3), and Paul's claim to have had what sounded very much like out-of-body experiences (2 Corinthians 12:1–6).

This is one of the places where the thinking of the European Enlightenment had a particularly profound impact on Christian beliefs. In the face of a dominant materialist view of reality, any worldview that had a place for the supernatural was soon relegated to the mythological dustbin as a hangover from a primitive and unsophisticated world that had apparently gone for ever. The dominance of this opinion in theology and philosophy in particular produced whole generations of church leaders who came to understand their own faith heritage in reductionist terms, and who regarded spiritual experience as little more than a branch of social anthropology, to be studied (if at all) only as a historical curiosity. For people who were also committed to a colonialist mentality, it was irrelevant to note that the majority of the world's people at all times and places have always believed in the mystical and the numinous. That just proved the superiority of the Western mind-set over the worldview of other races. The New Age has challenged all that. It has even, on occasion, argued that this loss of awareness of another world has contributed to the collapse of Western culture. Certainly, many people would agree with the sentiment attributed to C.S. Lewis, that 'It is since Christians have largely ceased to think of the other world that they have become so ineffective in this one.'

Looking to the Future

It has been claimed that the forces represented by the New Age 'represent the single greatest opportunity and the single greatest threat the church of Christ has faced since apostolic times'.[21] The nature of the threat should be obvious. For the New Age is tuning in to the legitimate concerns of people for the new millennium, and is addressing itself to widely felt human needs in a way that is widely regarded as more plausible than whatever the church may be offering. Probably a majority of New Agers have at some time in their lives been a part of the church, and have left it. They frequently leave because it seems that their spiritual needs cannot be met by what goes on there. In a survey of the beliefs of young people, George Barna discovered widespread evidence of the failure of Christians to address questions about spirituality, to the extent that the church is increasingly being perceived as not even interested in God. The comments of a 20-year-old say it all:

I honestly tried the churches, but they just couldn't speak to me. I'm not against churches or religion. I just don't want to waste

*my time in places that have no real wisdom, only to discover
that when I'm fifty or something. All I want is reality. Show me
God. Help me to understand why life is the way it is, and how I
can experience it more fully and with greater joy. I don't want
the empty promises. I want the real thing. And I'll go wherever
I find that truth system.*

He subsequently records the opinion of a 23-year-old who told
him: 'Sure, I believe in God, but I don't know what churches have
to do with knowing God. It's for another time, another mindset.'[22]

The church is losing ground and apparently has little of
relevance to say to today's spiritual searchers. It will be an uncomfortable experience, but Christians have to face up to the fact that
people are apparently being discouraged in their search for the
truth by what goes on in many of the churches they visit. Ironically, there is ample evidence that people today are more open to
the spiritual than they have been at any time for perhaps a hundred
years or more. There are some searching questions to be considered. Why is it that when people need healing – whether personal,
emotional or physical – they never think of the church? Why is it
that when they have a need to belong to a meaningful community,
the church is the last place they would go? Why is it that when they
are looking for ministry to their emotions they prefer altered states
of consciousness? Why is it that when they want someone to stand
alongside them, to touch them and to affirm them in some
physical bodily kind of way, they steer clear of Christians? The conclusion seems irresistible: maybe there is some truth in the New
Age belief that the church is not part of the solution because it is
also part of the problem.

At the same time, the New Age is undoubtedly presenting the
church with a great opportunity. Underlying all the hype is a profound search for the meaning of life. In an earlier chapter the New
Age was compared to a vacuum cleaner, picking up an eclectic

assortment of spiritual goodies. As subsequent chapters have shown, the variety is seemingly endless, as people move constantly from one thing to another in the never-ending search for answers that will satisfy. But whether through the exploration of past lives, or contacts with spirit guides, or the tarot – or any number of other therapies and beliefs that have not even gained a mention here – the same themes are constantly bubbling to the surface. Much of it might seem like unfamiliar and threatening territory for traditional Christians. But in reality, the New Age is raising the very same questions as we find in the opening pages of the Bible. How is it that a world which ought to be a place of peace and harmony has become so seriously flawed? In order to share the biblical answer to that, Christians will find themselves forced to use some unfamiliar materials, as they pick up images from the surrounding culture and use them to explain the Gospel. They will also find themselves in some strange places, for if New Age people are to hear the Christian message, the one certain thing is that they will not go to church buildings, which means Christians will have to go to where they are.[23]

Western civilization is in a state of flux which, because of the impact of globalization, is also affecting the entire world. The scientific-materialist philosophy that has dominated for the past two or three hundred years is finished. It still staggers on in some conservative institutions, but it has no real future. To the extent that Christianity has aligned itself with that view, it too has no future, as demonstrated by the rapid decline of traditional mainstream Christianity in Europe and North America. All the signs are that the emerging worldview will be a renewed supernaturalism, perhaps something like the New Age mixture. As I have sought to demonstrate, this has huge flaws, both ontologically and morally, whether in its religious guise, which is the New Age, or in its secular guise, which is postmodernity. If this is the best we can do, then civilization is not in a period of change: it is in a state of terminal collapse.

The reimagination of Christianity will involve a painful process of weeding out those aspects of the inherited beliefs that are little more than reflections of the secular culture of previous generations. It will demand some honesty about the mistakes that have been made. This generation might feel it is unfair to be required to make amends for things for which it was not responsible, but that will also be part of the package. Rediscovering the essence of biblical faith and contextualizing it in contemporary forms will not be easy. Those who try to do so will make mistakes, for which they will be condemned by other Christians. But they must press forward in the enterprise, secure in the knowledge that generations of Christians before them have engaged in the same struggles – and knowing that, at this time in history, this might well be the only last hope for the world and its people.

Notes

Preface

1 W.H. Clark, *The Psychology of Religion* (New York: Macmillan, 1958), 22.

Chapter 1 Mapping out the Territory

1 Fritjof Capra, an internationally renowned professor of physics in the University of California at Berkeley, is perhaps the most well known, and author of the New Age classic *The Turning Point* (London: Flamingo, 1983). Others in the same category would be Cambridge biologist Rupert Sheldrake, *The Rebirth of Nature: the Greening of Science and of God* (London: Century, 1990), and James Lovelock, author of the classic *Gaia: a New Look at Life on Earth* (Oxford: OUP, 1979). Lovelock is ambivalent about his personal commitment to the New Age philosophy, but his work has undoubtedly inspired much New Age thinking. Marilyn Ferguson, a psychology professor, has written the influential volume *The Aquarian Conspiracy* (Los Angeles:

J.P. Tarcher, 1980). For others, see William Bloom, *The New Age: An Anthology of Essential Writings* (London: Rider, 1991). The annual Festival of Body, Mind and Spirit, held in London each spring, has a seminar programme which is regularly addressed by people who are not only leading New Agers, but in significant positions within the British establishment – people like the late Sir George Trevelyan, the so-called 'father' of the British New Age, who was headmaster of Gordonstoun School (made famous when Prince Charles was sent there). The fact that many decision-makers, both in Britain and the USA, are committed New Agers, gives it significantly more influence than might be inferred from the actual number of New Agers in the community at large.

2   For an accessible account of the emergence of transpersonal psychology and its connections with the contemporary spiritual search, see R.S. Valle, 'The Emergence of Transpersonal Psychology', in R.S. Valle and S. Halling (eds), *Existential-Phenomenological Perspectives in Psychology* (New York: Plenum Press, 1989), 257–68.

3   For an example of such formal promotion of New Age values, see *TSBeat* issue 9 (1990), the youth magazine of the TSB, which gave its readers 'nine reasons that explain why New Age is good, is right and ready for now', and then asked, 'Could you get into New Age?', and gave an address to write to!

4   For examples of this approach, cf. Constance Cumbey, *The Hidden Dangers of the Rainbow* (Shreveport LA: Huntington House, 1983); Alan Morrison, *The Serpent and the Cross* (Birmingham: K and M Books, 1994).

5   J.L. Simmons, *The Emerging New Age* (Santa Fe: Bear and Co., 1990), quotations from pages 7, 12, 14.

6   Kenny Kaufman, quoted in *San Francisco Chronicle*, 25 April 1990.

7   Hemitra Crecraft and Sue King, interview with *The Philadelphia Inquirer*, 7 January 1990.

8   Shirley Maclaine, *Out on a Limb* (London: Bantam, 1987), 140.

9   Carol Riddell, *The Findhorn Community: Creating a Human Destiny for the 21st Century* (Findhorn: Findhorn Press, 1991), 64.

10   For examples of all these, see typical New Age magazines such as *New Age Journal* or *Kindred Spirit*. Barbie channelling was advertised in San Francisco's *Common Ground* 72 (1992), 80.

11   The Spiritual Rebel, whose thoughts can most easily be accessed through his web-site: http://www.wgn.net/~arhata/yes

12   L. Wittgenstein, *Philosophical Investigations* (Oxford: Blackwell, 1968), sections 65–78.

13   Elliott Miller, *A Crash Course on the New Age Movement* (Grand Rapids: Baker, 1989), 14.

14   Cf. Marilyn Ferguson, *The Aquarian Conspiracy* (London: Paladin, 1982), 231–41; Michael York, *The Emerging Network* (Lanham MD: Rowman and Littlefield, 1995), 324–34; Michael York, 'The New Age in Britain Today', *Religion Today* 9/3 (1994), 14–21.

15   Carol Riddell, *The Findhorn Community*, 222.

16   Carol Riddell, *The Findhorn Community*, 63.

17   Cf. C Sugden (ed.), *Death of a Princess* (London: Silverfish, 1998), especially my article 'The Death of a Princess: Lessons for the Church', 29–48.

18   See the Church of Diana web-site: http://www.dianaspeaks.org/

19   A recent example of such a phenomenological approach
      would be John Newport, *The New Age Movement and the
      Biblical Worldview* (Grand Rapids: Eerdmans, 1998). As an
      encyclopedic account of the diversity of popular Western
      spirituality today, it could hardly be bettered – but when
      everything becomes 'New Age', then ultimately nothing is,
      and the concept becomes meaningless.

20   Aldous Huxley, *The Perennial Philosophy* (New York:
      Harper, 1944); Robert Ellwood, 'How New is the New
      Age?', in *Perspectives on the New Age*, ed. J.R. Lewis and
      J.G. Melton (Albany NY: SUNY Press, 1992), 59; cf. also
      the article 'New Thought and the New Age' by J.G.
      Melton, in the same volume, 15–29.

21   Lawrence Osborn, *Angels of Light?* (London: Daybreak,
      1992), xii.

22   On postmodernity more generally, see Walter Truett
      Anderson, *Reality Isn't What it Used to Be* (San Francisco:
      Harper and Row, 1990); David S. Dockery, *The Challenge
      of Postmodernism: an Evangelical Engagement* (Wheaton IL:
      Bridgepoint, 1995); David Harvey, *The Condition of
      Postmodernity* (Oxford: Blackwell, 1989).

23   Cf. Paul Heelas, 'The New Age in Cultural Context: the
      Pre-Modern, the Modern and the Post-Modern', *Religion*
      23/2 (1993), 103–16.

24   E. Gellner, *Postmodernism, Reason and Religion* (London:
      Routledge, 1992), 22.

25   Fritjof Capra, *The Turning Point*, xvii. See also Capra's work
      The Tao of Physics (London: Fontana, 1976).

26   For one opinion on this, see Lesslie Newbigin, *Foolishness to
      the Greeks* (Geneva: WCC, 1986) and *The Gospel in a
      Pluralist Society* (London: SPCK, 1989). But there is more
      than a grain of truth in the New Age analysis. Cf. the
      comment of David Bebbington: 'It is extremely hard to

resist the conclusion that the early evangelicals were immersed in the Enlightenment. They were participating fully in the progressive thought of their age.' ('The Enlightenment and Evangelicalism', in *The Gospel in the Modern World*, ed. M. Eden and D.F. Wells, Leicester: IVP, 1991, 76).

27   Shirley Maclaine, *Going Within* (London: Bantam, 1990), 99; a view put forward with some vigour (and scientific insight) by Fritjof Capra, *The Web of Life* (London: HarperCollins, 1996).

28   For an informed account of neo-paganism, see Graham Harvey, *Listening People, Speaking Earth: Contemporary Paganism* (London: Hurst and Co., 1997). There is a good deal of debate as to whether this really is a rediscovery of the past, or whether it is not an imposition on the past of a modern agenda. See, for example, discussions of the allegation that Christianity (= 'patriarchy') displaced an original goddess-centred matriarchal culture: Mary Jo Weaver, 'Who is the Goddess and where does she get us?', in *Journal of Feminist Studies in Religion* 5/1 (1989), 49–64; Sally Binford, 'Are Goddesses and Matriarchies merely figments of feminist imagination?', in *The Politics of Women's Spirituality*, ed. Charlene Spretnak, (Garden City NY: Doubleday, 1982), 541–9.

29   David Spangler and William Irwin Thomson, *Reimagination of the World* (Santa Fe: Bear and Co., 1991), xvi.

30   Starhawk, *The Spiral Dance* (San Francisco: Harper and Row, 1989), 214.

31   *The Findhorn Community*, 63, roman type mine.

32   For a corrective, see Paul Greer, 'The Aquarian confusion: conflicting theologies of the New Age', *Journal of Contemporary Religion* 10/2 (1995), 151–66.

33   G. Trevelyan, *Operation Redemption: a Vision of Hope in an
     Age of Turmoil* (Walpole NH: Stillpoint Publishing, 1985).

Chapter 2 What is the New Age?

1   *The Whole Person* (Santa Barbara CA), July 1998, 11, 39.
2   Marilyn Ferguson, *The Aquarian Conspiracy*, 30.
3   'The members speak: what does "New Age" mean to you?',
     New Age Journal (November–December 1987), 52.
4   Sir George Trevelyan, 'Spiritual Awakening in our Time', in
     W. Bloom (ed.), *The New Age: an Anthology of Essential
     Writings* (London: Rider Publications, 1991), 33.
5   William Irwin Thomson, *From Nation to Emancipation*
     (Findhorn: Findhorn Press, 1982), 52.
6   Jose Arguelles, 'Harmonic Convergence, Trigger Event:
     implementation and follow-up', *Life Times Magazine* 3, 65.
7   Ian Wray, 'Buddhism and Psychotherapy', in G. Claxton
     (ed.), *Beyond Therapy* (London: Wisdom Publications,
     1986), 160–61.
8   Fritjof Capra, *The Turning Point* (London: Flamingo,
     1983), xvii.
9   Marilyn Ferguson, *The Aquarian Conspiracy*, 125, 142.
10   Ziauddin Sardar, *Postmodernism and the Other* (London:
     Pluto Press, 1998), quotations from 225 and 13.

Chapter 3 'Going Within'

1   Shirley Maclaine, *Out on a Limb* (London: Bantam, 1987),
     140, 327–8.
2   John Carman, in *San Francisco Chronicle*, 28 April 1988.
3   Shirley Maclaine, *Out on a Limb*, 215.
4   The pioneering work on the two hemispheres of the brain
     was carried out by Roger Sperry, who won the 1981 Nobel
     Prize in Physiology and Medicine for his research. Cf. his
     early paper, 'Brain Bisection and Consciousness' in *Brain*

and Conscious Experience, ed. J. Eccles (New York: Springer-Verlag, 1966). For an accessible survey of subsequent research, see Sally P. Springer and Gertz Deitsch, *Left Brain, Right Brain* (New York: Freeman, 1993, 4th ed.).

5　Shirley Maclaine, *Out on a Limb*, 198.

6　Marilyn Ferguson, *The Aquarian Conspiracy*, 380, 101.

7　On some of these particular movies, cf. Robert Short, *The Gospel from Outer Space* (London: Fount, 1983). For more extensive consideration of some of these themes, see Clive Marsh and Gaye Ortiz (eds), *Explorations in Theology and Film* (Oxford: Blackwell, 1997).

8　Russell L. Ackoff, *Creating the Corporate Future* (New York: John Wiley and Sons, 1981), 19.

9　R. Scott Peck, *The Road Less Traveled* (New York: Simon and Schuster, 1978), 281, 283.

10　*Bhagavad Gita* 2:46

11　M. Murphy and R.A. White, *The Psychic Side of Sports* (Reading Mass.: Addison-Wesley, 1978), 5–6.

12　For a more considered view of religion and sport, see S.J. Hoffman (ed.), *Sport and Religion* (Champaign IL: Human Kinetics Books, 1992).

13　Marilyn Ferguson, *The Aquarian Conspiracy*, 101.

14　Ted Peters, *The Cosmic Self* (San Francisco: Harper SanFrancisco, 1991), 55, 56.

15　Cf. June Singer, *Seeing through the Visible World: Jung, Gnosis, and Chaos* (San Francisco: Harper and Row, 1990); R.A. Segal, *The Gnostic Jung* (Princeton NJ: Princeton University Press, 1992).

16　*Gospel of Thomas* logion 77.

17　A. Guillaumont, H-Ch. Puech, G. Quispel, *et al.*, *The Gospel According to Thomas* (Leiden: Brill, 1959).

18   J.M. Robinson (ed.), *The Nag Hammadi Library in English* (New York: Harper and Row, 1977; revised edition San Francisco: HarperCollins, 1988).

19   htttp//www.epix.net/~miser17/Thomas.html

20   George Trevelyan, *Operation Redemption: a Vision of Hope in an Age of Turmoil* (Walpole NH: Stillpoint Publishing, 1985).

21   Shirley Maclaine, *Going Within* (London: Bantam, 1990), 30.

22   *Gospel of Thomas* logion 114.

23   See, for example, Bill Kerrell and Kathy Goggin, *The Guide to Pyramid Energy* (Santa Monica CA: Forces, 1977); C. Staniland Wake, *The Origin and Significance of the Great Pyramid* (Savage MN: Wizards Bookshelf, 1973).

24   A Valentinian slogan, reported in Clement, *Excerpta ex Theodoto* 78.2.

25   The organization calling itself the *Ecclesia Gnostica Catholica* is quite different from the groups described here, and consists of groups that continue the kind of magically based spirituality associated with Aleister Crowley (1875–1947).

Chapter 4 Searching for the Unknown

1   For the full story of Ramtha, see J.Z. Knight, *A State of Mind* (New York: Warner Books, 1987).

2   *A Course in Miracles* (New York: Foundation for Inner Peace, 1975).

3   Jane Roberts, *The Seth Material* (Englewood Cliffs NJ: Prentice-Hall, 1970); *Seth Speaks* (Englewood Cliffs NJ: Prentice-Hall, 1972).

4   Richard Bach, *Jonathan Livingstone Seagull* (London: HarperCollins, 1994).

5   B. McWaters, *Conscious Evolution* (Los Angeles: New Age Press, 1981), 111–12.

6   Shirley Maclaine, *Out on a Limb*, 209.

7   Shirley Maclaine, *Out on a Limb*, 187.

8   Stephen Hawking, 'Foreword' in Lawrence Krauss, *The Physics of Star Trek* (San Francisco: HarperSanFrancisco, 1995), xii–xiii.

9   J. White, 'Channeling: a Short History of a Long Tradition', *Holistic Life Magazine*, Summer 1985, 22.

10 M.J. Crowe, *The Extraterrestrial Life Debate 1750–1900* (Cambridge: Cambridge University Press, 1988), 547.

11 Cf. Alice Bailey, *Initiation, Human and Solar* (New York: Lucis, 1922); *The Reappearance of the Christ* (New York: Lucis, 1948).

12 J.Z. Knight, *A State of Mind*, 11–12.

13 Shirley Maclaine, *Out on a Limb*, 136.

14 J.L. Simmons, *The Emerging New Age* (Santa Fe: Bear and Co., 1990), 69–70.

15 *The Emerging New Age*, 83.

16 C.S. Lewis, *The Screwtape Letters* (New York: Macmillan, 1943), 32–3.

17 J.L. Simmons, *The Emerging New Age*, 95.

18 Carol Zaleski, *Other World Journeys* (New York: Oxford University Press, 1987), 205.

19 J.L. Simmons, *The Emerging New Age*, 117.

20 Ziauddin Sardar, *Postmodernism and the Other* (London: Pluto Press, 1998), 260.

21 R.C. Zaehner, *Our Savage God: The Perverse Use of Eastern Thought* (New York: Sheed and Ward, 1974), 71–2.

22 Richard Smoley, 'Fundamental Differences', *Gnosis* 14 (Winter 1990), 50.

23 J.L. Simmons, *The Emerging New Age*, 61.

24 Robert Monroe, *Journeys out of the Body* (Garden City NY: Anchor Books, 1973), 138–9.

25 J.L. Simmons, *The Emerging New Age*, 78.

26   Alice Bailey, *The Problems of Humanity* (London: Lucifer Press, 1947), 115–27.

27   David Spangler, *Revelation: the Birth of a New Age* (Findhorn: Findhorn Publications, 1976), 10–11.

28   Margaret Brearley, 'Matthew Fox: Creation Spirituality for the Aquarian Age', *Christian Jewish Relations* 22 (1989), 48.

Chapter 5 Healing – Ourselves and Our Environment

1   Marilyn Ferguson, *The Aquarian Conspiracy*, 267.

2   Shirley Maclaine, *Dancing in the Light* (New York: Bantam, 1985), 8.

3   Jill Ireland, *Life Wish* (Boston: Little, Brown and Co., 1987), 77.

4   R.C. Fuller, *Alternative Medicine and American Religious Life* (New York: Oxford University Press, 1989), 119–120 (roman type mine).

5   George Bush, *Mesmer and Swedenborg* (New York: John Allen, 1847), 160.

6   A.T. Still, *Autobiography of Andrew T. Still* (Kirksville MO: 1897), 99.

7   A.T. Still, *Journal of Osteopathy* (May 1894), 1.

8   R.W. Trine, *In Tune with the Infinite* (New York: Thomas Crowell, 1897), 16.

9   J.H. Kellogg, *The Living Temple* (Battle Creek: Good Health Publishing Co., 1903), 40.

10   P.P. Quimby, *The Quimby Manuscripts* (New York: Thomas Crowell, 1921), 180, 319, 173.

11   S.C. Hahnemann, *Organon of the Rational Art of Healing* (New York: E.P. Dutton, 1913), 102.

12   A. Fritsche, *Hahnemann, Die Ideem der Homoeopathie* (Berlin: 1944), 263–4.

13   D.D. Palmer, *The Chiropractor's Adjustor* (Portland OR: Portland Printing House, 1910), 821.

14 B.J. Palmer, *Do Chiropractors Pray?* (Davenport, Iowa: Palmer School of Chiropractic, 1911), 25.

15 G.F. Reikman, 'Chiropractic', in *The Holistic Health Handbook* (Berkeley: And/Or Press, 1978), 171–4.

16 *The Holistic Health Handbook*, 17.

17 Alice Bailey, 'Esoteric Healing', in William Bloom (ed.), *The New Age: an Anthology of Essential Writings* (London: Rider, 1991), 88.

18 John Keel, *The Eighth Tower* (New York: Signet Books, 1975), 16.

19 Korra Deaver, *Rock Crystal: the Magic Stone* (York Beach ME: Samuel Weiser, 1985), 40.

20 S. Thomson, *Boston Thomsonian Manual* 3 (15 November 1837), 21.

21 D. Kreiger, *The Therapeutic Touch* (Englewood Cliffs NJ: Prentice-Hall, 1979), 13.

22 R.C. Fuller, *Alternative Medicine and American Religious Life*, 99.

23 A. Maslow, *Toward a Psychology of Being* (New York: Van Nostrand Reinhold, 1968, 2nd ed.).

24 J.L. Simmons, *The Emerging New Age*, 158–9.

25 C. Myss, 'Redefining the healing process', in Bloom (ed.), *The New Age: an Anthology of Essential Writings*, 86–7.

26 L. Hay, 'Disease and Thought Patterns', in Bloom (ed.), *The New Age: An Anthology of Essential Writings*, 96–9.

27 J.L. Simmons, *The Emerging New Age*, 79.

28 M. Ferguson, *The Aquarian Conspiracy*, 253–4.

29 A. and O. Worrall, *The Miracle Healers* (New York: Signet Books, 1969).

30 Cf. D.R. Groothuis, *Unmasking the New Age* (Downers Grove IL: InterVarsity Press, 1986), 56–70. For a more considered Christian account of the matter, see John P. Newport, *The New Age Movement and the Biblical Worldview* (Grand Rapids: Eerdmans, 1998).

31   John Harris, *New Age: A Christian Response to a Serious Challenge* (Barton ACT: Zadok Institute, 1991), 5.

32   J.L. Simmons, *The Emerging New Age*, 161.

33   Editorial in *Watercure Journal* (12) 1852, 12.

34   M. Duke, *Acupuncture* (New York: Pyramid House, 1972), 164.

35   Cf. James M. Lovelock, *Gaia: A New Look at Life on Earth* (Oxford: Oxford University Press, 1979).

36   Dorothy Maclean, quoted in Paul Hawken, *The Magic of Findhorn* (London: Fontana, 1988), 146.

37   For more on this, see my article 'Defining a Biblical Theology of Creation', *Transformation* 10/2 (1993), 7–11; Michael S. Northcott, *The Environment and Christian Ethics* (Cambridge: Cambridge University Press, 1996).

38   Richard Smoley, 'Fundamental Differences', *Gnosis* 14 (Winter 1990), 50–1.

Chapter 6 Getting It All Together

1   Katao Ishii, *The Ultimate Super Will Power* (Gardena CA: ESP Science Research Institute, 1986).

2   The words of Rachel Storm, 'Disciples of the New Age', *International Management* (March 1991), 42–5.

3   A. Huxley, *The Perennial Philosophy* (New York: Harper, 1944).

4   C.A. Raschke, *The Interruption of Eternity* (Chicago: Nelson-Hall, 1980), 42.

5   Donald W. McCormick, 'Spirituality and Management', *Journal of Managerial Psychology* 9/6 (1994), 5.

6   For more extensive documentation of such cases, see J.R. Lewis and J.G. Melton (eds), *Perspectives on the New Age* (Albany NY: SUNY Press, 1992), 127–35; Richard Roberts, 'Power and Empowerment: New Age Managers and the Dialectics of Modernity/Postmodernity', *Religion Today* 9/3 (1994), 3–13.

7   Russell Ackoff, *Creating the Corporate Future* (New York:
    Wiley, 1981). The quotations are from page 13.

8   L. von Bertalanffy, *General System Theory* (New York:
    George Brazillier, 1968); *Perspectives on General System
    Theory* (New York: George Brazillier, 1975).

9   For a New Age interpretation of these trends, written by a
    scientist, see Fritjof Capra, *The Web of Life* (London:
    Flamingo, 1997).

10 *Creating the Corporate Future*, 25–6.

11 *Creating the Corporate Future*, 19–20.

12 *Creating the Corporate Future*, 19.

13 See, for example, Kennon Callahan, *Twelve Keys to an
    Effective Church* (San Francisco: HarperSanFrancisco,
    1983), *Effective Church Leadership* (San Francisco:
    HarperSanFrancisco, 1990); or R. Paul Stevens and Phil
    Collins, *The Equipping Pastor* (Bethesda MD: The Alban
    Institute, 1993), the sub-title of which is 'A Systems
    Approach to Congregational Leadership'.

14 *Creating the Corporate Future*, 6.

15 *The Aquarian Conspiracy*, 24.

16 Norman Vincent Peale, *The Power of Positive Thinking*
    (London: Mandarin, 1990; originally 1952). Peale's ideas
    owed much to Transcendentalism and New Thought,
    though he himself was in the mainstream of the Christian
    tradition. Cf. Carol V.R. George, *God's Salesman: Norman
    Vincent Peale and the Power of Positive Thinking* (New York:
    Oxford University Press, 1994). Others who have formed a
    bridge between the two would include the proponents of
    'prosperity theology'. Cf. Benny Hinn, *The Anointing* (Lon-
    don: Word, 1992), Kenneth Hagin, *How to Write Your Own
    Ticket with God* (Dallas: Rhema, 1979). For critical analysis
    of this movement, cf. J.A. Matta, *The Born Again Jesus of the
    Word-Faith Teaching* (Bellevue WA: Spirit of Truth, 1987,

2nd ed.); J.R. Lewis and J.G. Melton, *Perspectives on the New Age* (Albany NY: SUNY Press, 1992), 14–29.

17   *The Aquarian Conspiracy*, 352.

18   William H. Kautz and Melanie Branon, *Channeling: The Intuitive Connection* (San Francisco: Harper and Row, 1987), 136–7.

19   Barrie Dolnick, *The Executive Mystic* (New York: HarperBusiness, 1998), xvi–xvii.

20   *The Executive Mystic*, xvii.

21   *The Executive Mystic*, xviii, 31.

22   *The Executive Mystic*, 154.

23   *The Executive Mystic*, 146.

24   *The Executive Mystic*, 10.

25   *The Executive Mystic*, 121–4.

26   *The Executive Mystic*, 11.

27   *The Executive Mystic*, 37.

28   For all these things, see *The Executive Mystic*, 33–63.

29   *The Executive Mystic*, 203–26.

30   *The Executive Mystic*, 94.

31   *The Executive Mystic*, 105.

32   For these, and other examples, see *The Executive Mystic*, 173–4.

33   *The Executive Mystic*, 10.

34   *The Aquarian Conspiracy*, 118.

35   For books on management written from the perspectives of mainline religions, as distinct from the New Age, see the following. From a Hindu perspective: J. Hawley, *Reawakening the Spirit in Work: the Power of Dharmic Management* (San Francisco: Barrett-Koehler, 1993); Christian: J. Cowan, *The Common Table: Reflections and Meditations on Community and Spirituality in the Workplace* (New York: HarperBusiness, 1993); T. Chappell, *The Soul of a Business* (New York: Bantam, 1993); R.J. Banks, *Faith*

Goes to Work (Bethesda MD: Alban Institute. 1993); Zen Buddhist: L.G. Boldt, *Zen and the Art of Making a Living* (New York: Arcana, 1991), A. Low, *Zen and Creative Management* (Tokyo: Charles E. Tuttle, 1976); Jewish: R.E. Tauber, *I Shall Not Want: the Torah Outlook on Working for a Living* (Monsey NY: Shalheves, 1990).

Chapter 7 What is the New Age Saying to the Church?

1   Lawrence Osborn, 'The Gospel in the New Age', *Gospel and Culture* 18 (Autumn 1993), 1–5.

2   Irving Hexham, 'The Evangelical Response to the New Age', in J.R. Lewis and J.G. Melton, *Perspectives on the New Age* (Albany NY: SUNY Press, 1992), 152–63. Quotations are from pages 159 and 161.

3   For examples of this approach, see Constance Cumbey, *The Hidden Dangers of the Rainbow* (Lafayette LA: Huntington House, 1983); Alan Morrison, *The Serpent and the Cross* (Birmingham: K and M Books, 1994).

4   The same comment could be made of the propensity of some Christians to see the New Age as essentially an occult movement. While some traditionally occult practices are undoubtedly followed by some New Agers, this is a tiny proportion of the entire movement (I would estimate that less than 10 per cent of it falls into this category).

5   M. Ferguson, *The Aquarian Conspiracy* (London: Paladin, 1982), 146.

6   For more on this, see my *Faith in a Changing Culture* (London: HarperCollins, 1997).

7   Catherine L. Albanese, 'Religion and the American Experience: a Century After', *Church History* 57 (1988), 337–51, identified the following features that she believes are common to the New Age and to Christian fundamentalism: (1) Personal transformation and direct

spiritual experience, paralleled by the transformation of society; (2) Hearing voices is more important than seeing visions – a kind of mysticism expressed as ongoing revelation; (3) Healing: physical health and material prosperity as signs of blessing; (4) Ontological positivism, linked into religious materialism (biblical literalism on the one hand, literal reincarnation on the other); (5) A non-elitist do-it-yourself spirituality. See also Phillip C. Lucas, 'The New Age Movement and the Pentecostal/ Charismatic Revival: Distinct Yet Parallel Phases of a Fourth Great Awakening?', in *Perspectives on the New Age*, ed. Lewis and Melton, 189–211.

8   On post-evangelicalism, see Dave Tomlinson, *The Post-Evangelicals* (London: Triangle, 1995); Graham Cray *et al.*, *The Post Evangelical Debate* (London: Triangle, 1997); David Hilborn, *Picking up the Pieces: Can Evangelicals Adapt to Contemporary Culture?* (London: Hodder and Stoughton, 1997). For Matthew Fox's story, see his autobiography, *Confessions* (San Francisco: HarperSanFrancisco, 1996); and, for a brief treatment of the controversial issues he raised, R.J. Bauckham, 'The New Age Theology of Matthew Fox: a Christian Theological Response', *Anvil* 13/2 (1996), 115–26.

9   Though he probably never intended to do so, this is effectively the position put forward by David F. Wells in his book *No Place for Truth: or Whatever Happened to Evangelical Theology?* (Grand Rapids: Eerdmans, 1993). For a judicious assessment of this, together with discussion of other more open engagements with postmodern culture, see Millard J. Erickson, *Postmodernizing the Faith* (Grand Rapids: Baker, 1998).

10   See 'Salvation and Cultural Change', in D. English (ed.), *Windows on Salvation* (London: Darton, Longman and

Todd, 1994), 166–80; 'Christians, New Agers, and Changing Cultural Paradigms', *Expository Times* 106/6 (1994–5), 172–6; *Faith in a Changing Culture* (London: HarperCollins, 1997), 174–202; 'The Death of a Princess: Lessons for the Churches', in C. Sugden (ed.), *Death of a Princess* (London: Silverfish, 1998), 29–48.

11 Bhagwan Shree Rajneesh, *I am the Gate* (New York: Harper and Row, 1977), 18.

12 *Out on a Limb*, 210.

13 *Out on a Limb*, 215.

14 *Out on a Limb*, 41.

15 Ian Wray, 'Buddhism and Psychotherapy', in G. Claxton (ed.), *Beyond Therapy* (London: Wisdom Publications, 1986), 160–61.

16 The classic work here is Matthew Fox, *Original Blessing* (Santa Fe: Bear and Co., 1983). See also his 'Spirituality for a New Era', in Duncan S. Ferguson (ed.), *New Age Spirituality* (Louisville: Westminster/John Knox Press, 1993), 196–219. Fox has been rightly criticized for his simplistic rewriting of Christian history, and there is no question that the answers he gives to his own questions are quite unsatisfactory. But the questions remain, and will need to be addressed.

17 For detailed examination of all these issues in relation to the Bible, see Aida Besancon Spencer *et al.*, *The Goddess Revival* (Grand Rapids: Baker, 1995).

18 R. Ackoff, *Creating the Corporate Future*, 26.

19 *Creating the Corporate Future*, 44.

20 For specific examples of this in the Gospels, see my *Faith in a Changing Culture*, 82–107, 218–23.

21 Os Guinness, 'The impact of modernization', in J.D. Douglas, *Proclaim Christ until He Comes* (Minneapolis: Worldwide Publications, 1990), 283.

22   George Barna, *Baby Busters* (Chicago: Northfield, 1994),
     quotations from pages 93 and 143–4.
23   For a creative account of what this might involve, see Ross
     Clifford and Philip Johnson, *Sacred Quest* (Sutherland
     NSW: Albatross, 1995).